G000131019

Reasons to Live

Rikki Beadle-Blair

TEAM
ANGELICA

Published by Team Angelica Publishing November 2012
an imprint of Angelica Entertainments Ltd

Team Angelica Publishing
51 Coningham Road
London W12 8BS

www.teamangelica.com

A CIP catalogue record for this book is available from the
British Library.

ISBN 978-0-9569719-2-0

Printed and bound by Lightning Source.

About the author

Rikki Beadle-Blair was born and raised in South London. He attended the Bermondsey Lampost Free School where he could study whatever he liked and so focused on the arts and entertainment. He makes films, theatre, music, dance and art. His production company Team Angelica has developed several plays and films, including 'Bashment', 'Fit', 'KickOff', 'Taken In' 'Gutted' and Angelic Tales New Writing Festival. In 2011 he founded Team Angelica Books with Co-editor-in-chief John R. Gordon. Passionate about encouraging creativity and self-expression, Rikki has developed several courses under the 'In the Room' banner to facilitate creative career advancement.

Contact: rikki@teamangelica.com

This for all the beautiful boys and girls of every colour
and shade

and every sex

from Butch to Butterfly

who have considered suicide

When this rainbow is enuf.

I've heard it said that youth is wasted on the young.

I say it's wasted on those who tell themselves they're old.

Whatever your age, this is your youth.

We will never be this young again.

This book is about embracing our youngness.

Fully

Wholeheartedly

Bravely

This book is about seizing our life.

This book is for the young.

The animal wise.

The wild.

The restless.

The peace-seekers.

This book. Right here. In your hand. Is for you.

Stay young.

Reasons to Live #1

There are angels everywhere, in everything, in everyone. The best way to see one is to be one. It's the same
with devils. When we acknowledge our own demons,
we shed light on the hell that others live in and the
gates to humanity swing open. We don't have to
condone, we don't have to forgive. But the power is
there to extend a hand and lead the world to freedom.

Reasons to Live #2

No matter what you tell yourself, this day belongs to
you. You've cultivated this routine and are able to step
out of it any time. True liberation lies in allowing
yourself to see that you're exactly where you choose to
be and this life is yours to maintain or change. You can
relax and accept, bide your time and make plans or rise
up right now and rebel. Your day, your life, your choice.

Reasons to Live #3

A day to try something new, a day to conquer a problem, a day to fall short before sitting down to work out why. A day to get up with the sun, a day to lie in. A day to call someone you miss - a day to start learning something new that you've always wanted to. A day to replace one bad habit with a good one. A day to create. A day to mourn. A day to finish. A day to begin. A whole day.

Reasons to Live #4

You cannot be accurately compared with anyone because you are incomparable. This cluster of molecules is a singular miracle. Only you can ever live this story at this time, in this unrepeatable sequence. Only you can gather and share your particular chemistry of wisdom and love. Your potential contribution is unparalleled and invaluable. Compare yourself to no one. You are a unique gift to the world.

Rikki Beadle-Blair

Reasons to Live #5

Creative spirits travel offbeat pilgrim paths. The more intrepid you are, the lonelier you can feel. But there are kindred spirits eager to travel with you - perhaps your paths are already entwined. Don't mask your creativity to blend with the crowd. You will only feel lonelier. If you let your maverick soul run free, the world will respect you, and your kindred will find you. Believe.

Reasons to Live #6

You are surrounded by untapped genius. Co-workers, bosses, employees, your lovers, family and friends, even 'enemies' and total strangers are all brimming with brilliant ideas, creativity and truths. They may not be aware of inspiration they offer. It may even be opposite from their intent - but put your ego aside and listen to your life's landscape and you will sail a sea of epiphanies.

Rikki Beadle-Blair

Reasons to Live #7

You, like the universe, are constantly expanding; growing, learning and teaching. You, like the world, are multi-faceted, multi-cultural, steadily evolving. You, like all humanity, are capable of epic self-destructiveness and heart-stopping creativity. You, like every family, are worth fighting for. You, like any scared delinquent child, deserve your patience, understanding and love.

Reasons to Live #8

You don't have to take yourself so seriously. You can pursue your passions, fall flat on your face in dog dirt and if you just roll onto your back and laugh out loud to the skies, all embarrassment will evaporate. Any great free-runner will tell you a little humiliation is good for you. Get up and gratefully tend to your wounds, then get back to the serious business of having fun.

Rikki Beadle-Blair

Reasons to Live #9

You don't need everyone's permission or approval. Craving mass acceptance is the enemy of creativity. Pandering to popular taste leads to the death of innovation. Make your contribution to evolution, listen to the murmurs of your rebellious blood and bones, and be your bravest and boldest and most beautiful. Dazzle the cynics, inspire the timid, enlighten the indecisive and do your brilliant thing.

Reasons to Live #10

Everything that happens to you - joyous or brutal - is another invitation to an awakening. Each day life reveals itself as a tutor offering another opportunity for you to open your eyes, shake off the sleep of helplessness, reach out to seize the day, and take your turn at the wheel. Use your knowledge. Decide on a destination, choose a direction, delay your adventure no longer; start steering.

Rikki Beadle-Blair

Reasons to Live #11

The romance you crave is now. You are the leading man or lady in this movie. Stop waiting on bouquets and start sending, stop wishing for love letters and start writing, stop dreaming of the grand gesture and make it. Drop everything and grab this chance to appreciate life's staggering beauty, starting with your own. Romance yourself 'til you become a love song and then serenade the world.

Reasons to Live #12

Your body is not a cage. There is no right way to be masculine or feminine, there's only your way. Boy, girl or dolphin, you belong. What's sexier than someone girly and ballsy or blokey and tender? Change tyres in a tutu, pirouette in bike-boots, choreograph your own ballet, be as soft or strong as only you can be. When you tear up the rule-book and live in truth and honesty you liberate the world.

Rikki Beadle-Blair

Reasons to Live #13

There is nothing to truly fear. Maybe just a little: that tiny tug in the gut that says, 'Here we are on the rollercoaster'; that feeling that reminds you you're no longer cosy at home on the sofa searching for the remote - you're out there in the world taking your life into your hands. That healthy little taste of terror that comes with throwing your head back and drinking the juice of life.

Reasons to Live #14

When you make the decision to focus on health - physical, mental and emotional; when you dare to take an honest look at what you allow into your body and brain; when you let go of the over-processed and the artificial and focus on what's organic and real - in body and soul - that's the day you really start to thrive and begin to come alive. A day of refusing all poison. It starts with one day.

Rikki Beadle-Blair

Reasons to Live #15

No one will ever entirely know you. You are too wide a continent for anyone to cross. You're a human jungle, alive with surprises, populated with bold chameleons and shy butterflies. You are unfurling like a flag, a bud exploding in slow-motion. You are a series of revelations, an unfathomable mystery. You are a new galaxy and this is just your beginning.

Reasons to Live #16

Mistakes are cause for celebration. Slip-ups come with bold strides; sweet fruit is born of bitter seeds. I hope I make a hundred mistakes today; I pray that I learn that many lessons. A life without experiment is a breathing death. I cannot be defeated, only taught; criticize me and I am compelled to do my best and better. Watch me fall and rise unvanquished to forge further and beyond.

Rikki Beadle-Blair

Reasons to Live #17

You need depend on no-one for appreciation or understanding - though it is lovely when it comes. Pledge your energy to real progress, direct your ambitions, explore your capacity, improve your skills to expand your strengths. Self-confidence requires self-appreciation and understanding. Become an expert in yourself and see how swiftly anxiety evaporates.

Reasons to Live #18

You are a freak of nature. A glorious and strange cosmic surprise. Whether accidental or intentional, your conception changed lives and your birth transformed the constellation of humanity. You don't have to justify your singularity. Dance your dance as gratefully and generously as you can and your contribution will be obvious. Your riches, however modest, make the world wealthy.

Rikki Beadle-Blair

Reasons to Live #19

Those goose-bump moments when your vision of existence connects with another's - when the shared spark lights up everything and the possibilities in every direction seem infinite. Those moments of connection and chemistry that re-ignite your romance with the world, when you realize that you are not - and never were - alone. Those moments when we are illuminated by love.

Reasons to Live #20

Life, like every other romance, requires passion, commitment, constancy, creativity and appreciation. Invest complete involvement and you'll reap rewards. Share your strength and sensitivity and you'll be your most attractive. Stride with confidence and partners will fall in step. Send flowers, give compliments, offer support, take an interest. Make others feel special - and you will be special.

Rikki Beadle-Blair

Reasons to Live #21

There's more to sleep than recovery from the day. There's more to waking up than just sitting up in bed. There's more to mornings than hangovers. No intoxicant can match the rush that comes with clarity. Facing reality as it is brings the rush of realising that whatever your history or current situation you are mighty enough to face it as yourself, with nothing more than your courage, your honesty, your unclouded wits and your wide-open eyes and arms.

Reasons to Live #22

Find a way to dance a little every day, in public or private. Tap a foot, bob your head, make love, sprawl in the grass, stretch. Forget 'skill', find your own style and groove and just move. The sillier or scarier that sounds the more you need it. If you are breathing you have rhythm, the beat is waiting there in you, grace is flowing through your veins. Unzip your skin and release yourself.

Rikki Beadle-Blair

Reasons to Live #23

Pursuing purpose doesn't have to be painful. It's a matter of perspective and shifting your reward system. Healthy, nourishing eating can be a delicious treat, keeping fit an invigorating celebration. Committing to your passions will transform your working life. Don't waste another moment choosing suffering, choose glamour over grind and relax into the love of life you were born with. Live fully. Live now.

Reasons to Live #24

If you are prepared to apply yourself consistently and persistently you can move mountains. The key is to find mountains worth moving. Parroting popular values will leave you empty and despairing. Forget luck; the bigger the dream, the harder you'll need to work. Choose work that's meaningful and life will be too. Know why - decide how - start now.

Rikki Beadle-Blair

Reasons to Live #25

Existence is a mystery. Purpose doesn't need to be. Exploring options and investigating our impulses are all delicious gifts to feed and fill our empty days. When we relish self-investigation, and learn to love questions as much as answers, this big beautiful world is ours again. Explore life on foot, grateful for every step, appreciating the climb that earns you the view. Own your journey, own the world.

Reason to Live #26

Joy is a choice. We can decide to be happy, regardless of the weather, location, circumstance or relationship we're in. We can shift whenever we want - if not geographically then psychologically, which is the one that truly counts. And that shift starts with being appreciating who are you and your opportunities. Constant dissatisfaction can be a sly kind of complacency. Try ambitious satisfaction. Choose joy, seize life.

Rikki Beadle-Blair

Reasons to Live #27

When we lose people on our journey, that loss, that memory and that love urges us on to Live: bear witness, pay tribute, declare our love for those who have moved on, chosen different roads or stopped to rest. Love is our spur, love is our fuel, love is our inspiration - the pain and passion and the mystery of it. Until it's our turn to lie down, we stand up. Love Love Love = Live Live Live.

Reasons to Live #28

So much music to make, so many steps to take, moves to explore, picture to paint, stories to tell, parts to play, words to learn, words to say. Life is what we make it - and each day I learn more and more that we can make anything - ANYTHING we want. We are each the human miracle that leaves this universe and all we encounter in it changed. And that epic legacy is a reason to truly Live.

Rikki Beadle-Blair

Reasons to Live #29

There's always another chance. Another chance to make a change, to make new choices, to say sorry, to offer and accept love, to embrace responsibility, to understand, to create romance, to make amends, to escape, to break the chain, to see the truth, to tell the truth, to reassess, to rebuild, to be reborn. Give yourself a chance to live. Give the world a chance to be wonderful.

Reasons to Live #30

This whole world was given to you on arrival and you are owed nothing more. Your capacity for gratitude and giving is tested with every inhalation. If you can spend your time here in appreciation of all this beauty - including your own - and a willingness to understand yourself and your universal family; if you can offer all you have and ask for nothing, you will reap the miracle.

Rikki Beadle-Blair

Reasons to Live #31

Whether you unfurl like a bud on a bough, or flower like a firework in the sky, if you can find a way to expand every morning and share your light and your hue, your own way to claim your place as one of nature's wonders, you will make your way from being a wanderer to becoming a destination, an aspiration, an ambition. Stop dreaming. Stop hoping. Become hope. Become the dream.

Reasons to Live #32

Realism is useful, but only when you create and customize your own reality. Building a path entirely out of other people's limited visions and fears will take you through wasteful draining jungles to unwelcoming deserts where you will become disoriented and lost. We can learn so much from others, but the truest teacher is the heart that pulses in you. Follow that beat and you will find your course, your freedom and true satisfaction.

Rikki Beadle-Blair

Reasons to Live #33

By all means review your life, but don't torture yourself. Okay, you've done what you've done; said, eaten and tried some stuff that didn't work for you. Learn your lessons but channel your main energy into today's move - the move that will take you from disappointed to dynamic, from survivor to achiever, from dreamer to visionary. Progress takes belief. Give yourself your faith, give yourself your best.

Reasons to Live #34

The toddler we all once were, who picked up the brush without fear and began to paint. Who made friends with everyone in the playground without labelling, offering instant friendship with no dread of 'networking'. Who spoke the truth without fear, who sang, danced and played any character without inhibition or a union card. This is the Artist we all want to be - the child prodigy you and I really are.

Rikki Beadle-Blair

Reasons to Live #35

The greatest success is to live one's life freely without fear of failure. The greatest triumph is to discover and maintain our true character in a world full of distractions. The greatest courage lies in the strength it takes to truly be ourselves regardless of whether it makes us popular or acceptable. These are the greatest riches: clarity, integrity, independence, courage, humanity and love.

Reasons to Live #36

It's more than possible to be honest and open - it's essential. Even as we embrace our education, it's vital to remember that our harvest of knowledge has been gathered from one perspective and others around us have their own truth. Before we dismiss an 'opponent's' point of view, why not explore it, dig in and mine it for all it can offer us? It's so much more valuable to grow wiser than to win.

Rikki Beadle-Blair

Reasons to Live #37

There is no 'secret'. The path to success is simple and obvious: Identify what makes you come alive, channel as much of your energy towards that as you possibly can without reservation or hesitation, then share that passion lovingly and freely with everyone you meet without waiting for permission. Success is a river of clarity, intention, freedom, generosity and love. Dive in.

Reasons to Live #38

Listen to yourself. The first step to freedom lies in identifying your true voice, so often obscured by the cries in your head that tell you what you should look like, what you should fear and what you should own. I believe yours is the gentle voice that firmly announces your equality to all creation, reminding us that all you need to do is take back possession of yourself. That you own this day. That this life is yours.

Rikki Beadle-Blair

Reasons to Live #39

Life is change - whether that means progress is entirely up to you. Before you speak, eat or to commit to any action, develop the habit of asking yourself these quick questions: Is this healthy? Is this honest? Is this progress? Is this kind? You are the sum total of your choices. Life is an accumulation of choices. Your decisions will become your destiny. Decide who you want to be.

Reasons to Live #40

Empathy. Nothing is more enlightening or liberating than the ability to experience the world from another's perspective. Through their eyes evil employers become struggling shipwreck survivors and difficult parents become scared children playing dress-up. With empathy we transform ourselves from the wounded to the healing, from the bewildered to the understanding, from the tiny hell of 'Poor Me' to a wide world of Us.

Rikki Beadle-Blair

Reasons to Live: #41

Freedom. The day I finally grasped the startling con-
cept that NO-ONE could make EVER me do
ANYTHING I do not want to do; that every decision in
my life - even under threat or torture - is always ultimately mine; all the suffering, fearful walls around and
within me began to melt, leaving me ready to deal with
each challenge and choice as what and who I truly am
and always will be until my last conscious breath: A
free man.

Reasons to Live #42

Your smile. Whether facing a stranger, a lover, an
enemy or your own reflection, one smile changes
everything. Your icebreaker, game-changer, mood
elevator and most effective weapon. It's how you
melted hearts the day you were born, it's the key that
can open doors today – around you and inside you.
Sometimes smiling takes strength. Build your soul
muscle, lift everyone's spirits. Happy beats petty every
time. Joy is the most coveted commodity. Own it.
Smile.

Rikki Beadle-Blair

Reasons to Live #43

Your strength. When it all falls apart around you there is that core of calm and control within you to call on, a store of wisdom and clarity and focus that can see you through any crisis. This is your best self. This is your inner lion. If you know yourself and are willing to show yourself, you can meet any challenge. If you know how to sail your ship, you need have no fear of storms.

Reasons to Live #44

Growth. If we can let go of trying to be everyone else – while still gathering inspiration from everyone we encounter – with each passing day we can grow wiser, kinder, more perceptive, more understanding, more independent, more sensual, more practical, more beautiful and, if we can just find it within us to treat ourselves with kindness, honesty and consideration, we can grow younger. Life is wonderful. We are wonderful. Look in the mirror and say Wow.

Rikki Beadle-Blair

Reasons to Live #45

Inspiration. Instead of looking for ways to tame the world – ways to hide from the sunlight and the storms, or to control others and the environment in order to find the happiness we seek - we can go to the wild natural place inside us that was there before we put shoes on our souls and began to crave things we don't need. We can trust our barefoot naked selves to provide our own happiness. We can allow those around us to teach us with their wisdom and their failings. We can let life inspire us.

Reasons to Live #46

You matter. What you say, what you do, even what you think, is food for the world. Those who love you, those who fear you and those who do not notice you are affected by your mood and reflect your presence. You are a contribution. You are a saving grace. You are an achievement. You are a prize. Be gracious with the fragility of others and pay tribute to our potential by choosing to be the best you can manage to be. Because you are a representative of humanity. You are the world.

Rikki Beadle-Blair

Reasons to Live #47

You can do anything. Anything that you truly madly deeply want to. What's needed above all is clarity. If you are clear and pure in your intention, clear and certain as to your goal's achievability, and clear and honest as to your level of commitment, mountains can be scaled. Start with the self-made mountains inside. Know that you are as powerful as you decide to be, as effective as you deign to be and as inspiring as you are determined to be.

Reasons to Live #48

Don't waste another moment wishing you were someone else, somewhere else, doing something else. You're not. You're right here, right now and everything you wish to become is within your grasp. You simply have to commit to yourself and do what needs to be done. It's not easy, but it is simple. Begin by accepting the fact that your life will not live itself. It needs to be inhabited. Leap into your body, take possession of your journey and announce the astounding story of you.

Rikki Beadle-Blair

Reasons to Live #49

History is a teacher not a ruler. The past has no power over you other than what you give it. You are not defined by your experience, but by your interpretation of it. Use what your family and schooling gave you to get stronger, softer, kinder and ever more certain of yourself. You are so much more than your sad stories. More than the sum total of events so far. You are the world's future, as yet unwritten, waiting on your poetic, practical contribution and unique signature.

Reasons to Live #50

Whether you succeed or fail, if it's as someone else, you will still be unfulfilled, you will still be lost. If before taking any action we asked, 'Will this take me towards myself or further away?' what might change? What would we eat, say and wear? Where would we choose to work? Who would we marry? You deserve to be happy. The world deserves the real you. Step towards yourself and refuse to step away. That is how you will make this world better and how you will truly come alive.

Rikki Beadle-Blair

Reasons to Live #51

You are the white knight you've been waiting for. The saviour who can step in and change everything. No need to wait for another moment. The cavalry is here. The rescue party is you. Pick yourself up, love yourself, encourage yourself, lift yourself to safety. No more poor me, no more conspiracies and supervillains, just the thrill of facing the truth and taking action. Don't keep your true identity a secret. Swoop in and save your world. Use your super strength, your super vision and fly.

Reasons to Live #52

It's not how others see you that defines your self-esteem, but how you see yourself. Don't look for your worth in the fickle marketplace, but in your own natural confidence and abundance. Making others accountable for your feelings can transform words into grenades and admirers into torturers. If you wish to be understood and appreciated, strive to understand and appreciate. It's not how the world approaches you that can change your life, but how you approach the world.

Rikki Beadle-Blair

Reasons to Live #53

You need envy nothing, because you are part of everything. Everything beautiful and brilliant around you is within you like a seed waiting for the sun's encouragement. The movie star's glowing smile, the athlete's passionate velocity, the self-made mogul's drive to rise and strive. The criminal's misguided selfishness is in you too - waiting for your empathy to ignite and guide you to kind choices. Humanity is yours. Make the most of it and it will make the most of you.

Reasons to Live #54

As long as we have consciousness, we have creativity. When we abandon the victim voice and embrace our artist's eye, imagination ignites. Abusers become muses, wounds become ideas, our blood calls out for the canvas and brush and we see inspiration in everything. Today is clay, waiting for our hands. The deeper we have to dig the higher we can build. The darker the night gets the brighter we can shine. Let's build a gallery in the ghetto and send an open invitation to the world.

Rikki Beadle-Blair

Reasons to Live #55

You don't need to weigh less to step lightly. You don't need to weigh more to be powerful. You don't need cash to be rich or approval to be valuable. You don't need compliments to be pretty. You don't need to have sex to know you're sexy. You don't need darker skin to look sleek, you don't need lighter skin to light up. You don't need music to dance. You don't need to dance to be funky. You don't need bouquets to take a bow. All you need is what you have. All you need is you.

Reasons to Live #56

My body needs more love not more discipline. My body needs nurture not guilty 'treats'. Junk food is not reward, it's punishment. Fat is my body trying to make the most of episodes of abuse. Skin problems are not a betrayal but a cry for help. Stuffing then starving my body and bribing it with sugar is cruelty in denial. Loading my body with poison then forcing it to achieve excellence is deluded and barbaric. But it's not too late. My body is ever-faithful and will respond to love.

Rikki Beadle-Blair

Reasons to Live #57

Relax. If you want to swim faster, run further, dance better - relax. If you want to digest your food, process your thoughts, make the most productive choices - relax. If you want relationships to flourish, when you want conflicts to be resolved and you need colleagues to calm down, chill out and focus on progress. It's time to lead the way and demonstrate freedom from tension. Diminish stress, banish fear, bring back romance and fun. Breathe in, breathe out... Relax.

Reason to Live #58

We live the life that we believe is ours. Not the one we dream of. Not the one we've been told we're capable of or deserve, but the life that we believe in enough to demand of ourselves. The limitations others put on us mean nothing unless we accept them. When we decide to silence the scared voices that make us cynical and lazy; when we refuse to accept anything less than a life of passion and commitment; when we can finally see how simply incredible we are... We're ready.

Rikki Beadle-Blair

Reasons to Live #59

You've survived it all and here you are, reading these words, still alive, ready to realise that your strength is staggering. And there is still time, right now in this moment, to decide what you're going to do with all you've learned from your mistakes and the thwarted expectations of others. Their weaknesses are available to help build your ability to evolve and prosper from all that life offers. And you know it's there - because here you are, still breathing. Alive and living.

Reasons to Live #60

Every time you stop caring what others think of you, you come alive and start having more fun. You dance where you want, you dress how you want. Your voice, your walk, your laughter and choice of lover are all liberated. This is not selfishness, this is generosity. It does not benefit the world for you to reduce yourself to fit its expectation. Offer honesty with sensitivity. Share your fresh idea. Give yourself without reservation - and help set us all free.

Rikki Beadle-Blair

Reasons to Live #61

Each day you declare your true intentions to the world. If you're unsure of your purpose, it's right there in what you are prepared to commit to, not occasionally, but regularly. If you want to know who you really are, look at what you are driven to sacrifice, what you feel compelled to risk. Whatever you want to believe, this daily announcement is loud and clear to everyone: 'This is what matters to me. This is the life I choose. This is the love of my life.' The world is at your feet. Waiting for your next step. Step bravely, step wisely, step tenderly, step freely. Send out an invitation to the world to join your dance.

Reasons to Live #62

There's nothing quite like that feeling of finding a new mountain to climb - standing at the foot of something you're about to make possible. If you want to know what makes you feel alive, find something that humbles you. Seek out what daunts you and get it done, get it said, defy yourself and be yourself in the same breathless bound. Nothing is bigger than you except you. Nothing can get the better of you besides you. You're the mountain. Conquer yourself.

Rikki Beadle-Blair

Reasons to Live #63

There are no endings, only beginnings. Evolution is eternal and essential. So things and people haven't gone the way you wanted them to? Every brick wall you hit houses a doorway to freedom. Open the door and see what's beyond. Don't be blinded by stale desire. Don't stay stuck in disappointment. Don't demand, demonstrate. Don't insist, inspire. Let go of your desire to control the world and seize each new chance to control yourself. Change is inevitable - what are you going to become?

Reasons to Live #64

The only path to freedom is through yourself. It begins with realising that you are not a slave to the past or future. Nor to systems, conventions or expectations or fear. If others govern you it is because you choose to capitulate. But you can choose revolution at any moment. Wherever you are. You can rise up and reclaim your life. Stop waiting for freedom to be granted. The responsibility is too great for the rest of us to bear. Liberate yourself and you liberate us all.

Rikki Beadle-Blair

Reasons to Live #65

Unlock the chains of your expectations. Release yourself from the cage of betrayal and disappointment. Free your mind to focus on what's actually real, present and available. Invest your energy in what can be achieved instead of chasing shadows and daydreams. Opting to feel cheated leaves you ragged and helpless. Turning the unexpected to your advantage makes you an inventor and alchemist.

Reasons to Live #66

Every passing second brings the offer of something new. New opportunities, ideas, angles. You can be someone new, go somewhere new, change your tactics or your priorities. If you are ever stuck it's in your head. Your limits are just stories you tell yourself. You can create a new story right now. Script it, cast it, design it, choose the soundtrack. If it doesn't rely on someone else's green light you can start rolling on your schedule. Be exactly who you want to be. Take the lead. Call action.

Rikki Beadle-Blair

Reasons to Live #67

You don't have to accept the way anyone else sees you. You can decide how to present yourself to yourself. You can transform how you feel about who you are by simply telling the truth. How can a mum be 'single' if she has her child with her? Why not be an Independent Mum? Take all those words like 'broke' 'lonely' 'minority' or 'disabled', decide what's useful and what's in your way and focus on the only truth that matters - That you are as wonderful as you permit yourself to be.

Reasons to Live #68

Get out of your own way. Allow the creativity to flow, allow opportunity to present itself, allow the love to bloom. No one can block your pathway the way you can. And no one can free you except you. Let go of the foolish need to feel perfect every moment. Experience your infant self being a little clumsy as you learn to walk, inept as you learn your skill, out of tune as you search for your key. Relax, thaw, shift, expand, grow, advance. Get over yourself.

Rikki Beadle-Blair

Reasons to Live #69

This is your life in action. Who you are, where you live and who you live with are not ideas, they're choices with consequences you're already living by. You can plan to make changes on Monday. But until Monday comes those changes don't exist. Whatever you plan for the future, why not act on it now? This moment is yesterday's future. Time to revise what went wrong, what went right and what never went. What can you do to put your passion into practice? What are you waiting for?

Reasons to Live #70

Everywhere around there are moments of grace, hiding in the quiet folds of the day. Shy in the shadows. Connections with strangers, new discoveries within old friends, shafts of sun that set you aglow. Even in those thought of as lost and irredeemable there are flashes of kindness - unpredictable creativity - arresting revelations - valuable inspiration - a love that makes innocents of cynics. And they are there in you, even at your clumsiest - these moments of grace, waiting on your attention and your faith.

Rikki Beadle-Blair

Reasons to Live #71

The only review that will change your career is your own. The only declaration of love that can make you feel beautiful is yours. That life-changing call will come from you. The only prize worth winning is your confidence. You are your own winning ticket, you are your own jackpot. There is one ruler in your kingdom and the rest are pretenders. Give yourself the only raise that will make you rich. Stop waiting for the phone to ring and start calling. Stop praying for miracles and step onto the water. Trust yourself. Own yourself. Free yourself.

Rikki Beadle-Blair

Reasons to Live #72

Your 'enemies' need understanding; every envious insult, every desperate attack, every self-hating blow is a tribute to your achievements. Your body needs appreciation; every honest pound of flesh, every educational lump and bump, every unique spot and scar. Your mistakes need celebrating; they are your toddling children - the evidence of your courage and proof of your youth. Your chores need the warrior in you to seize and convert them into joyful daily achievements that propel you into the loving heart of life. You have no weaknesses, just lovely vulnerabilities that stand testimony to your strength. You have no flaws. Just wild things to feed with love.

Rikki Beadle-Blair

Reasons to Live #73

Lines on your face will not make you old; worrying about wrinkles will rob you of your youth. Greed will starve you, giving up will defeat you, fear will paralyse you, self-obsession will isolate you, laziness will exhaust you, demanding to receive love before you give love will leave you lonely. All that you want from life will spring from you when you allow it to flow. When you give up being the bucket and become the well, the earth will flock to you and you will be forever young and rich, brimming with abundance, glimmering with promise, gleaming with hope.

Rikki Beadle-Blair

Reasons to Live #74

You cannot be free by seeking freedom. But only by letting go. You cannot be free through fighting for freedom, only by accepting it. Freedom is not money or the power of flight. Freedom is in the appreciation and acceptance of any situation, whatever its flavour or market value. Freedom is being able to live life exactly as it is before concerning ourselves with change. Freedom is allowing love and understanding to flow through you wherever you are or whoever you're with. Freedom is the willingness to be truthful without judgement, to be generous without fear of poverty, to be loving without need. Freedom is gratitude. Freedom is love.

Rikki Beadle-Blair

Reasons to Live #75

You set your own limits. If you want to dance, you can, regardless of your shape and size and health. If you're paralysed, start blinking and teach the world a new rhythm. If you're tone-deaf and want to sing, get wailing, whining, growling. Your voice is valuable, write your own melody, create your own scale. Don't get trapped by age, history, heritage, or location. Don't let anyone tell you what you're capable of. Show them what all of us can do if our spirit is willing. Defy society and gravity. Demonstrate our universal freedom. Be a brain, be a body, be a beacon, be ridiculously various and fearless. I understand now - those who believe we live more than one life are right. Let's live them all today.

Rikki Beadle-Blair

Reasons to Live #76

The fragility of everything is part of its magic. Each moment is made fleeting to offer us the gift of urgency. Skin sheds, leaves fall, bodies dissolve - we transform, evolve - we move on. In moments of confusion or despair witness the impossibly complex simplicity of your skin, the miraculous science of air passing through your lung-tissue and realise that you - like a vein in a leaf, like a lash in a blinking eye, like a single heartbeat out of billions – are a tiny, crucial contributor to something heartbreakingly epic and beautiful. Feel everything. Let your heart break, let your heart soar and fill yourself with wonder. Let yourself be inspired, let yourself be inspiring. Let yourself be alive and keep moving.

Rikki Beadle-Blair

Reasons to Live #77

Whatever your struggles, the only one that matters is with yourself. And you can end that with a decision. Cease struggling and flow into action. Give up helplessness. Refuse to be poor. Dispose of frustration. Discard your fear of judgement. Decline to suffer through your day. Take the wheel, seize responsibility and admit that you are where you are because of the action you have taken and the choices you have made. Tap into your dynamism. Mine your creativity and your courage. Commit to being bold and brave. Channel your passion. Choose to be as rich and free as you actually are. Admit that you are beautiful. Claim your star. Decide.

Rikki Beadle-Blair

Reasons to Live #78

If you are lost it's because you haven't been paying attention. If you are stuck it's because you haven't resolved to move. If you're afraid, it's only of yourself. Who else has power over you? Look around at this wide world. Once you've decided where you want to be, head towards your destination without hesitation or apology. Pick up your pen, take up your instrument, get down to the track and run. You can dream about it all you want, but your real life is something you live. Become pen, become ink, become beats and chords, become a library and a living gymnasium; seize the earth in your bare hands and sow your seeds. Defy your history and commit to glory. Take flight and write your epic story across the sky.

Rikki Beadle-Blair

Reasons to Live #79

People will try to tell you how masculine or feminine you need to be in order to get stamped acceptable, but the truth is that all they are thinking about is themselves and where they stand, and what they hope will make them comfortable and accepted. The only thing you need concern yourself with is your truth and your own honest contribution to the constellation of humanity. Allow yourself to be who you are, with your own shifting combination of sun and moon, and cast your ever-changing light on who we all are. Do not fear your grace or your strength, your muscle or your magic, your swagger or your glide. Relax into yourself - your maleness, your femaleness, your fabulousness - and you will find comfort and true love.

Rikki Beadle-Blair

Reasons to Live #80

Choose your battles wisely - conflict is a huge drain on energy resources. Whenever you go to war, it's always ultimately with yourself. It's so much swifter and sweeter to go to peace with yourself. And to do that we have to seek the peace in everything - and everyone. And the search begins within. Releasing the calm that comes with the realisation that we are strong enough to let go of victory over others and the need to be admired or appreciated or even acknowledged by anyone but ourselves. We only truly win when others are no longer required to lose. The greatest victory is the freedom from ego and the terror it brings. Lose yourself in the liberation of setting your enemies free.

Rikki Beadle-Blair

Reasons to Live #81

Each day presents you with a series of beckoning doors; open opportunities to create, to explore, to question. Each door is made of glass, develop your focus and you will see where it leads. When you decide where you want to go you will know what to look for and what questions to ask - and your life will answer. Destiny is a wish, fate is a fairytale. The majority of journeys are decided by the nature of your desires and the quality of your choices. There are few universal keys to life, but one is this: You are the door - for others and for yourself. Open up.

Rikki Beadle-Blair

Reasons to Live #82

If you are true to yourself you can never be truly lost and you can never truly lose. Your brightness and beauty are in your hands alone. If others criticize, let them criticize your truth. If they are confused let it be your honesty that confuses. If they resist and reject, then let them resist and reject your fearless authenticity. Don't support society's lie that the road to acceptability is narrow or dark. It's as broad and clear as the air that connects us, as free and clear as you dare to be. Stand by nature's inventiveness and the treasures she has showered upon you. Teach the world how to appreciate itself by living, dancing, advancing and being the essence of self-acceptance and love.

Rikki Beadle-Blair

Reasons to Live #83

Look at yourself, the landscapes of your skin. Feel your uniquely graceful self in motion, the air swirling about you, caressing you in nature's appreciation. Listen to creation humming all around, calling you out of your shy cave into the unexplored galaxy that is continually gently insistently offering itself. You can be brave. You don't have to stay on the traditional path, you don't need to do what you've always done; you can be inspired by the past without being a slave to it. You can respect tradition whilst sculpting something new. You can spring forth from convention and venture into something radical and lovely. You can customize your adventure to suit your own evolving needs. You may do anything and be anything you feel you wish to be. It begins when you choose. Listen to the beat of your blood - how it calls and calls you to shamelessly dance to your unheard song. How it cries out to everything and everyone....Be New, Be True, Be You. Live, Live, Live.

Rikki Beadle-Blair

Reasons to Live #84

You can set standards. You can raise them. Avoid cliché. Avoid poisons. Avoid snobbery. Abandon fear. Choose love. Never procrastinate. Be polite when others are rude. Be loving when others are lazy, critical, hypocritical or cruel. Pay attention when people are showing you how screwed up they are. Don't be ruled by your neuroses. Be respectful when others are thoughtless. Listen to young people - even when you've heard it all before. When looking for love, be patient. When dressing in the morning, be authentic and brave. Eat breakfast and fuel the rocket. Surround yourself with teachers. Move on when others are afraid to. Don't waste energy on holding grudges. Be creative when others seem hell-bent on destruction. Never forget you are your own boss. Be kind.

Rikki Beadle-Blair

Reasons to Live #85

You can change the world. You already do. You smile and others light up. You are the landscape that others live in. When you change the way you treat yourself, you begin the chain reaction. When you pay loving attention to how you treat others, your life becomes a craft, your graciousness becomes a gift. When you move with purpose you become the epicentre of creative earthquakes with each step, and the world shakes with the thrill of you. When you morph from caterpillar to butterfly or from grub to moth, from each beat of your wings flows humanity's progress, sparking lightning-bolts of inspiration for all who encounter you. Your very existence creates change, and you can choose the kind of change you would like that to be.

Rikki Beadle-Blair

Reasons to Live #86

All around you, people are choosing the mundane path. But you can be the one who chooses the special. Take a real look at your life. What would it look like if you let go of everything other than what you really love or really need? What if you stopped ritually grinding and resolved only to earn the money you need through work you love? What if you stopped devouring through habit and taught yourself only to eat what you need and love? What if you stopped shopping mindlessly and only spent on things you love and need? What if you only wore clothes you loved? What if you finally paid attention to designing the day-to-day life you know you most need? Don't be afraid to show the world your true face. It may take them time to recognise the real you - but like any true love - you will know yourself at first sight.

Rikki Beadle-Blair

Reasons to Live #87

The world needs warriors. The world needs lovers. The world needs teachers. The world needs students. The world needs adventurers. The world needs innovators. The world needs mavericks. The world needs pioneers. The world needs artists. The world needs souls who feel compelled to stand up and be counted. The world needs spirits who help make others realise that they matter. You are all of these and so much more. You are awesome and the world needs you to stop wishing and whining and get on with your job of bringing our attention back to how perfectly designed we are. The world needs your inspired insanity and your everyday uniqueness. The world needs the global/ local/ individual revolutions that only you can instigate. The world is waiting. The world is waiting for you.

Rikki Beadle-Blair

Reason to Live #88

In the end it comes down to what you do. You can analyse and theorize, you can talk up your dreams and wish your life away, but your real life is constructed from what you actually get done. Criticize others all you want to, but when you die it won't be their achievements or failures that will flash before your eyes but your own. People can say what they like, but until they've done it, they're just voyeurs. Nothing tackles fear better than taking action. Nothing improves until something moves. If you want progress or change or happiness, only you can make it happen. Make a move.

Rikki Beadle-Blair

Reasons to Live #89

You are surrounded by stars. Friends, colleagues, acquaintances and strangers filled with talent, passion, ambition and love. Focus on those who are ready today to share their spirit and pursue fulfilment of their potential and the others will catch up later. Celebrate, support, encourage and bask in the brilliance of those who are prepared to let their light shine. Let them energise and inspire you, and give your unbridled appreciation and inspiration in return. Invest in our shared potential for lovely little moments of greatness. Offer your courageous faith up to humanity and that faith will be returned. No artist need be alone. Art lives in everyone. Let's each of us unveil our gleaming spirit and together we can encourage the fearful and hesitant to rise up and shine.

Rikki Beadle-Blair

Reasons to Live #90

Every day is another chance to dump your ego and get on with the business of falling in love with yourself. If you feel you could have a nicer face the best start is to smile. You can take your body to another level of fitness but you can't sustain it without appreciation. You can work on your skin, teeth, abs and hair, get wigs, weaves and implants, but if you're building on a foundation of disgust you're constructing a torture chamber of increasing disappointment. You can bully yourself and punish your poor faithful body, but bullies create a life of punishment for themselves. Why not stop starving yourself with self-criticism and put yourself on a diet of gratitude and faith? Why not stop mythologizing others and admit that you're a babe? Stop depriving the world of you. Let your foxiness run free.

Rikki Beadle-Blair

Reasons to Live #91

You don't have to conquer the world to own it. You only need acknowledge responsibility for your part of it. Tend your acre, work with the weather, plant your seeds wisely and waste no time on resenting the seasons. Be grateful for all you reap. It may not be what you hoped for, but whatever you have in your life is special, because you have nurtured it, and it will respond to your attention and appreciation. Be the first to admit that you have green fingers and a golden touch and the world will eventually agree and inevitably respond with its own miracles. But it all starts with you. So take the lead - let your clear bright eyes illuminate everything you encounter and light the way to the real victories - love unleashed and life unlimited.

Rikki Beadle-Blair

Reasons to Live #92

Few things are as overwhelming as success. The gutters of the world are filled with people who got what they wanted. The best way to be sure you're ready for paradise is to appreciate the journey it takes to get there. If you don't respect the field, you won't appreciate the harvest. Frustration is habit-forming, bitterness is addictive, suffering is a drug - if you don't indulge in it, you can't get hooked. Make gratitude your drug of choice, savour every hit, every trip, every twist and turn. Happiness takes practice, so does success. Learn to recognise it now and start getting used to it. Don't postpone your life. This is it. Plug yourself in and relish every electric second.

Rikki Beadle-Blair

Reasons to Live #93

There's a part of you that knows. Advance inwards into your deepest self and listen to the voices in the darkness. The pioneer voices, the inventors, the builders, the farmers, the hunters. Find the song of your gypsy - your true, wise, unbridled nature. Listen to that tune, trust it, follow wherever it leads. It's the voice that your fear rushes to crush, your ego shoves aside, your 'civilized' training teaches you to disregard with painful, repetitive, life-stealing consequences. The call in you to heal yourself, feed yourself, the urge to discover more, learn more, share more. The heart of you that sees that you, with all your sores and scars, are self-sculpted out of perfect clay - whatever others see or say. An instinctive spirit that understands that you may be domesticated but you can never be tamed; that you may be possessed but will never be owned. That you are the soul of freedom and no other can rule you. The part of you that exhorts your sleeping warrior to get up, get out, get going and return home with tales of legendary adventures. This is the whisper of the universe, addressing itself through you. Ignore it and you ignore life itself. Embrace it and you hold the key to everything anyone can ever achieve or be. There's a part of you that knows. Hear yourself. Heed yourself.

Rikki Beadle-Blair

Reasons to Live #94

The choices are simple. Self-pity or self-motivation. Tears or sweat. Anger or education. Frustration or gratitude. Drama or clarity. Dreaming or awakening. Wishes or action. Asking or offering. Passion or safety. Suffering or change. Judgement or understanding. Fear or love. Limitation or liberation. Fiction or truth. Fantasy or life. Maybe or must. Someday or today.

Rikki Beadle-Blair

Reasons to Live #95

Put aside your habits and listen to your instincts and you will know exactly what to do. Forget about your compulsions, honour your intuition and you will remember what's really best for you. You know who really gets you, who loves you and who you can count on. You know the way forward and you know the way home. Stop deluding yourself, let go of denial, stop pretending to be helpless, stop convincing yourself that you're lost. You know exactly what you need to learn, you know what you need to stop doing, you know who to stay away from, you know exactly what direction to go. Admit to yourself that you know what life you deserve and you know how to pursue it and stop hoping to dodge the work. Summon up your sleeping strength and determination, reconnect your sixth sense to your common sense and get back on track. Your real life is wonderful. But it's not waiting. Catch up before it gets away.

Rikki Beadle-Blair

Reasons to Live #96

It is not how you are treated by others that asserts your value in this world, but how you treat others. Are you respectful? Are you understanding? Are you even listening? Treating others the way we feel we deserve to be treated, meeting and maintaining our own standards, brings us something more enriching than status - it brings us integrity. This is not about giving license for others to exploit and misuse you. You can point out injustice and you can refuse to engage with negativity and you can choose to withdraw. And all of this can be done with grace, perceptiveness and even love. How you make others feel is ultimately how you make yourself feel. What kind of world do you want to live in? What kind of world are you willing to make?

Rikki Beadle-Blair

Reasons to Live #97

We fill our days with the search for distractions, busily manufacturing reasons to delay our journeys, banishing our visions to the stunted realm of dreams. But we are also free and able to put those distractions aside and seize our stories with both hands. There is no need to let your previous choices inhibit your next ones. It's never too late to take on new skills, expand our abilities, fulfil ambitions and forge new pathways in our brains and our lives. All that's needed is clarity and commitment to who we are and all we can be. Reschedule your days, restructure your life, reroute your path, begin your adventure.

Rikki Beadle-Blair

Reasons to Live #98

You can change the rhythm any time. If you don't like the way your life is going, or the way the river is flowing, you can change the course of things. Decline to be carried astray by your mistaken past choices, refuse to pander to other people's self-serving vision of you. Decide on your own journey, invent a fresh itinerary and venture off the tourist trail. Resolve to make your world spin your way. We deserve the benefit of the best of you and so do you. Don't hesitate, don't hold back. Set your course, set sail and sweep us all away to somewhere truly new.

Rikki Beadle-Blair

Reasons to Live #99

Be honest even when you know you won't get caught. Tell the truth even if no one seems to be listening. Keep your promises regardless of whether there are witnesses. Be your best self despite the fact you are the only one there. Few things are more demoralising than failing to meet your own standards; nothing is more futile than cheating yourself. Treat yourself the way you'd like others to. Offer yourself integrity, along with understanding and support. Gently insist on investing in a kind, consistent, healthy life and stake your claim in a stable, loving world.

Rikki Beadle-Blair

Reasons to Live #100

It's not about someday, it's about today. It's not about there, it's about here. It's not about them, it's about us. It's not about maybe, it's about must. It's not about could, it's about will. It's not just what you think, it's about what you believe. It's not about what you hear, but how you listen. Stop making excuses to the world and listen. Listen to the school in your gut that tells which of your instincts to trust. Look at yourself reflected in the sky and see how wide your real horizons are. Connect with every one of your senses and commit to your destiny. Listen to the wings of the eagle within as they beat against the cage of your ribs. The wide-winged spirit that insists and insists – '...Now. ....Now. ...Now.'

Rikki Beadle-Blair

Reasons to Live #101

If you want to build something that lasts, pay loving attention to the foundations. If you want clearer skin, better grades, smoother progress, solid relationships, a sharper mind... stop stressing yourself and start encouraging yourself, take note of your achievements, feed your self-esteem. You'll need it. Every time you rip yourself to shreds you tear up your roots, making your branches stunt and your leaves wither. This world belongs to everyone, but it's seized by the confident. Be supportive enough to be your own best friend. Be creative enough to be your own architect and start with the interior. Lay foundations of love and you can scrape the sky. Why not? It's your sky.

Rikki Beadle-Blair

Reasons to Live #102

So grateful that there's still so much to learn. What's more wonderful than this urge to keep questing, keep questioning, keep going, keep stretching, expanding, discovering, reorienting, understanding and gently demanding more of oneself. To take down the big top and move the circus on to the next town, the next show. Explore forests, deserts and ocean floors and continue the unfolding adventure. Artists as teachers and students, learning and sharing and confessing our innocence. Entertainers as investigative adventurers. Storytellers as scientists, geographers and detectives, excavating history and telling tales that explode and expand like fireworks to call the villagers of the world to huddle together round the campfire and wonder. What a life, what a life.

Rikki Beadle-Blair

Reasons to Live #103

Every tycoon knows that ownership is key. Never surrender your assets, never give away your copyright. Take possession of your life in every way. Assign no blame or responsibility to anyone. The day that you choose to joyfully assume total sovereignty over your choices and circumstances, you shake off your chains and you stand there as you were always meant to be: free and ready to stake your equal claim in this miraculous world. As powerful as the winds and oceans. Owed nothing by anyone. Your pockets full of offerings, all the treasures that you own. Free.

Rikki Beadle-Blair

Reasons to Live #104

All there ever really is love. It's all anyone ever cares about. They may confuse it with sex, mistake it for money, replace it with desperate, determined bids for power, but in the end it's love they hunger for, affection they crave, significance they seek. Every savage act, every unfathomable action can be explained when we see that our friends, foes and families are all wandering in the same forest searching for the same thing - that you can offer to everyone, freely at no cost. Carry crumbs of love in your pockets to calm the snarling beasts, prepare feasts of love and send out open invitations to all your starving relations. They may be afraid of approaching the fire, but warmth always wins. Offer the food of love and eventually everyone comes calling to dine.

Rikki Beadle-Blair

What I learned today #105

Look around at this thrilling spinning world. Give your attention to what makes you smile, what scares you awake but reassures you just enough. Channel your energy into what fills you up and fuels your engine. Insist on focusing on what ignites you: that's where you will find your next adventure and your safest refuge. That is where you will find the passion that makes sense of your adventure. That is where you will find what will feed and clothe you. This is where you will find yourself. This is where you'll find a sustaining lasting love.

Rikki Beadle-Blair

Reasons to Live #106

The revolution can commence whenever you decide. With your wholehearted commitment to the cause of freedom, all the oppressors in your mind who told you that brilliance belonged to someone else, that you were born the wrong shape or colour or in the wrong time or place to be who you want to be, are exposed as charlatans. If you decide that you have the strength, power and grace to carve out your own road you can cut through any mountain and offer emancipation to the weary slaves that surround you. You can be a gentle undeniable force in this world. Evolution is a given. Revolution is a decision. You can make your own world, make it turn a new way and make a beautiful brand new contribution - whenever you decide.

Rikki Beadle-Blair

Reasons to Live #107

Excuses will not solve your problems. Excuses will not feed you or free you. If you couldn't do what you said, you should have said something else. In the end there are two major factors that decide your life story - What you do and what you don't do. That's who you are, that's the life you're leading. If you don't drink you don't get drunk, and if you don't do the drug, you don't get hooked. If your spouse is holding you back, it's because you married them. If you're late you didn't leave early enough; if you're broke it's because you bought too much. It's not what you earn that makes you poor, it's what you spend. Don't play the blame game and claim a 'legitimate' excuse – you will fool no-one but yourself and you will be left with an excuse for a career, an excuse for a life. Your family is not an excuse, your neighbourhood is not an excuse, your age, your race, your face are not excuses. Excuses will crush your vision. Excuses will keep you weak. Excuses will make your life an untested theory. Excuses will turn reality into dreams – and you will never awaken and you will never live. No more excuses. Only action. Only life.

Rikki Beadle-Blair

Reasons to Live #108

Inspiring and inspired people are all around. You can seek out the company of those who believe in themselves enough to find time to believe in others. You can refuse to be dragged down by those who are defeated by their self-imposed limitations. You can decide to empathize without becoming overwhelmed yourself. You can love the tired and the lost while moving onwards and outwards into the world. There are peers and mentors who will encourage and support you. You can reach out to them with gratitude and generosity. You can encourage and support others. You can choose to be inspiring and inspired. You can inhale opportunity and share with the breathless. You can be fully in the world. You can be fully alive.

Rikki Beadle-Blair

Reasons to Live #109

You don't have to die to be reincarnated. A new life is available to you right now. Don't be afraid of who you really are. Encourage yourself do the work it takes to raise your standards. Remind yourself that as long as you are alive and alert, you're young enough to grow. Trust yourself. Choose yourself. Enjoy yourself. Be yourself. Right now.

Reasons to Live #110

It's not self-indulgent to focus on your strengths. It's not egotistical to offer up your talents. Why waste time? Be honest with yourself and everyone else about what you're good at. That's where your purpose lies. And, if you give yourself over to it wholeheartedly, where you will find a wealth of happiness to share.

Rikki Beadle-Blair

Reasons to Live #111

You are not stuck. Anytime you feel like you're not heading the right way you can stop, reassess, and change direction. Step out of the traffic. Go somewhere you can think, remember where you were going and where you wanted with all your heart to be, then consult your map, reset your sat nav and set off on your way again. Refuse to be mired, decline to be imprisoned. Pick up the child you were once and take them on that journey your promised. Let the others succumb to fear and insist on their traps. If you head towards what calls you it is never too late and you are never lost. When you're going where you truly want to, you're always on time.

Rikki Beadle-Blair

Reasons to Live #112

The issue is not whether you have ability. We are all gifted with some form of talent. The question is how you're going use it. Once you've found what fires you, then you need to find a way to channel it. When you connect your skill to a cause you will automatically, almost magically, generate passion and drive. Don't worry about what your assets will bring you, concern yourself with what they will bring others. Concentrate on a way to be of service and the energy that will flow through and from you will amaze and excite you beyond anything you can buy. There's no greater discovery than identifying your purpose.

Reasons to Live #113

In the midst of our pursuit of happiness we so often forget to have fun. Finding work, going to work, working itself, can all be fun. A sense of humour and a spirit of adventure can metabolise the mundane and make the everyday an adventure. You can decide to laugh more and help others to laugh with you. Wake up and take a fresh look at everything, your wardrobe, your neighbourhood, your friends, your family, your partner or your single life and investigate how you can make the best of it all... and the most of yourself.

Rikki Beadle-Blair

Reasons to Live #114

And each day the sun rises, burns through mist, sometimes sulking behind a veil of grey, sometimes darting shyly from cloud to cloud and sometimes standing proud and naked in the sky without fear or shame. Each day a different sun but always there, whether seen or unseen. So it is with love. Always there, in blue skies or grey. Always with us.

Reasons to Live #115

All the things you crave and covet - love, affection, encouragement, validation, significance - are already yours to give. Whether others are ready to accept it or not, if you offer the world the nourishment that you value, it is you who will thrive, it's you who will grow. In every act of generosity there is a fistful of seeds. Give up being needy and give away all you can spare and you will never be poor, you will never be hungry, you will never be alone. The cradle of life rocks in you.

Rikki Beadle-Blair

Reasons to Live #116

If you don't like your life, change the way you live. This is your party - you're the host and everyone in your life is the guest. If people are rowdy or rude, look at the invitation you've been sending out. Review your own behaviour - what tone are you setting? What have you taught them they can get away with? If you've got problems with gate-crashers or party poopers, graciously let them know what you're prepared to tolerate. If they persist, show them the door. Your party, your guests, your rules, your responsibility, your life.

Reasons to Live #117

Everything wonderful you've ever witnessed, every sweet taste and savoury tang - each act of kindness, gesture of friendship, startling achievement or stunning sky, has not passed or faded. Nothing lovely in your life is gone. It lives in you, ready to rise up and reveal itself and surprise you with your almost-forgotten history. Pay tribute to everything amazing in your world with your choices and add to the accumulation of beauty in this marvellous limitless world.

Rikki Beadle-Blair

Reasons to Live #118

Take a good look around - at the golden and the grey, the clouds and the blue. Check out the human body - curvy or lean, skin wrinkled or smooth, inky dark or alabaster pale. Observe our attempts and endeavours - reckless or considered, creative or destructive, point-less or wise. Hot or cold, hard or soft, gargantuan or microscopic - take a good look at it all and see yourself in everything and remind yourself how infinite and breath-taking you are.

Reasons to Live #119

You don't know your own strength. You are so much tougher, so much smarter, so much softer, so much gentler, braver, wiser, than you have allowed the world to see and you've permitted yourself to be. Every day is an invitation to explore the boundaries of your regions. The further you go, the wider your horizons. If you encourage yourself to be courageous, who knows where you might find yourself. Who knows where you could take us?

Rikki Beadle-Blair

Reasons to Live #120

Sometimes it's enough to love. Regardless of whether it's returned, appreciated or even noticed. To love without demanding or needing or controlling. To love enough to let others be free to love and live - with you, without you, beyond you. To realise that they have their life and you have yours: with, without and beyond. To remember that the purpose of love is to make us strong. Strong enough to offer it. Generous enough to receive it. Resilient enough to save it for those who are ready to share it. Brave enough to keep moving on until we find where we belong. Bold enough to love yourself, independent of the responses of others. Big enough to simply love.

Rikki Beadle-Blair

Reasons to Live #121

The call to live is never greater than when we lose others. That's when the drum inside us beats louder, urging us to turn up our flame and venture further into the darkness and light it up with our appreciation for those who have gone ahead of us. To rediscover their legacy in everything and share it with everyone. To work and play in celebration of their inspiration. To pay tribute to their lives by living. To stop wasting time being bitter, directionless, wilting, lazy, and half-awake - to become fully present, engaged, grateful, passion- ately-living testaments to the breadth, depth and strength of love.

Reasons to Live #122

True darkness is rare in nature. Even on cloudy moonless nights there is a corona around the horizon and the invitation is to trust in shadows and silhou- ettes. Relax, gently feel your way forward, knowing that there's a world full of sounds and scents to discover. Don't retreat further into the darkness, venture out of your cave, feel the night breeze on your skin. Experi- ence the dark. Insist on your adventure anyway.

Rikki Beadle-Blair

Reasons to Live #123

Every mistake brings us closer to each other. Our weaknesses keep us humble. Our failings help us understand our exhausted parents and overwhelmed teachers. Our frailty forces us to acknowledge our need for affection. Perhaps if we can treasure our vulnerability and share it without shame we will feel less need to find our strength in defeating others, and free up the precious time to explore the daunting, mysterious oceans that lie beyond our fearful shallows. Let's give up our desperate defences, our preening pride and petty victories and dare to discover how strong it makes us to survive being wrong. How freeing it is to face the little failures and still thrive.

Rikki Beadle-Blair

Reasons to Live #124

You are so much more brilliant than you think you are. However many formal diplomas you have or baffling exams you've flunked - however old you are, however young, no matter how dumb or pretentious you have been made to feel, your brain is crammed with mighty giants waiting to be reawakened and encouraged to dance. Look at all you have learned and are capable of learning, and know that you are a gleaming reservoir of untapped genius. Reawaken your brain, feed it, tone it up, loosen it, build its muscle, and eventually it will run, jump, pirouette and pack a punch. Pick up a book, visit exhibitions, enrol in classes, venture into nature, seek out peers who relish debate. Direct sunlight into your inner garden to grow brilliant flowers and plucky persistent weeds. Ignite your mind.

Rikki Beadle-Blair

Reasons to Live #125

Love is always an option. Always waiting, curled inside you like a feline sleeping in a tree, it can awaken anytime, leading you somewhere new, seducing you into rediscovering someone you encounter every day, inspiring you to fall in love again and again, building layers of tenderness. And it's waiting in others too. All around, you are being watched, appreciated, admired or desired. Little gusts of affection, hoping to blow your skirt up or your shirt open, aching for a fleeting moment of connection. Family, colleagues, carers or passing strangers, somehow, somewhere, you have caught someone's eye, and captured someone's heart. If you live you are loved. And capable of loving beyond measure or expectation.

Rikki Beadle-Blair

Reasons to Live #126

You are still so full of surprises. Inside you are vast unexplored regions, whole continents of potential. New perspectives to appreciate, new art to create. No one can ever entirely know you. No one ever needs to. Take your companions on a journey to your creative extremes. Show them their potential by fulfilling your own, as you bravely shift and change, stretch and evolve. Demonstrate that opportunities for expansion are infinite within all of us; that it's never too late to learn, to transgress our boundaries, physical and intellectual. Never believe the lie that you are fixed, complete, frozen, cooked, finished. Never accept that you are too old to learn or too young to achieve. Never believe that you cannot determine your own status quo. Why restrict yourself when you can amaze yourself? Pay tribute to the miracle of creation and create. Expound the theory of the big bang and expand.

Rikki Beadle-Blair

Reasons to Live #127

The wind you have to lean into, the sun that beats down, the chill that turns the world white overnight - these are not limitations designed to frustrate you. They are invitations: to skate, sail or fly a kite, to burrow under the blankets for a loving cuddle, to climb or roll down the nearest hill. To start a snowball fight with someone you long to touch, or lie in the sultry dune grass and gaze up thoughtfully or thoughtlessly at the endless blue. To try something unexplored in you and risk breaking a bone. To make yourself breathless or become serenely still. To embark on your latest investigation and let yourself feel the wild thrill surge through you that only surfing life's sudden opportunities can bring.

Rikki Beadle-Blair

Reasons to Live #128

No one else can make you happy. No one else is responsible for your responses to life's offers and challenges. You alone calculate the value of the events and people in your life. You alone can evaluate and capitalize on the opportunities before you. Others can point things out, only you can conclude what is useful. You decide what is beautiful and you decide what to do with it. You cannot make others love you, appreciate you or understand you and it's not healthy or helpful to try and force them to. It's exhausting to live and die by the responses of others all caught up in their own needs and insecurities. It's a waste of your life to try to force the world to react on cue. Freedom comes when we stop trying to control our surroundings and seize the prerogative to take control of ourselves. Commit to being useful. Commit to being helpful. Commit to being beautiful. And decide what to do with yourself.

Rikki Beadle-Blair

Reason to Live #129

Trying to make others feel bad in order to make ourselves feel good is entirely pointless. If it's sunshine you're after, why head towards the clouds? The swiftest route to feeling good is making others feel good. Stop chastising, focus on healing and start feeling better today.

Reasons to Live #130

You have a voice. It springs out of you with every gesture you make, every move you choose. You can choose to try and love everything, including yourself. You deserve to be heard. The world has the right to hear you. Listen to the world around you screaming, whispering, the stutter and flow - find your space and join the conversation. Speak up for love, speak up for kindness, speak out for the passion and freedom that lies beyond the procrastination of addictions. Create, construct, explore, share, sing out with all your unfettered, unaltered heart.

Rikki Beadle-Blair

Reasons to Live #131

Nothing is wrong in the world - just sometimes incon-venient. Nothing's off, nothing's unfair - it just is. Once you make the decision to commit to Life exactly as it is - embracing it as a blessing and seeing through the lazy illusion of what our lives could be like if they were not our lives... then immediately opportunity, like a sky-full of fireworks, lights up and re-colours everything.

Reasons to Live #132

When you let go of ego, people will praise you. When you stop suffering, people will empathize. When you get a sense of humour, people will take you seriously. When you admit your weaknesses, people will salute your strength. When you are generous, you will be showered with gifts. When you are grateful you will be blessed. When you admit that you know nothing, you will start on the road to wisdom. When you cease struggling, you will make progress. When you claim your independence you will find connection. When you are loving, you will be loved.

Rikki Beadle-Blair

Reasons to Live #133

Whenever you are unafraid of looking foolish, you find your courage and your grace. If you can live your life unfazed by criticism, determined to focus on what's helpful and practical, you will be emboldened to make giant strides. When you set yourself free of the fear of rejection, you will be ready to pursue your plans without distraction. The day you let go of the need to be seen as successful is when you will begin to triumph.

Reasons to Live #134

No enemies, only inspiration. No problems, only education. No dreams, only vision. No exhaustion, only satisfaction. No fear, only anticipation. No uncertainty, only options. No disasters, only opportunities. No frustration, only ingenuity. No bad luck, only perspective. No loneliness, only freedom. No shocks, only awakenings. No disappointment, only reality. No worries, only calls to action. No suffering, only choice. No loss, only life.

Rikki Beadle-Blair

Reasons to Live #135

Once you realise that almost your entire experience of life takes place in your mind and decide to take control of your thinking, you transform your existence. You decide what is beautiful. You determine what is valuable. You design your own pain and suffering. You define success. You don't need to impose this on others, and you don't have to bow down to what others try to impose on you. The key to happiness is simple and in your hands. Think independently and build your connection to the world from a calm clear peaceful place. A place that you have created. A place that is truly yourself.

Rikki Beadle-Blair

Reasons to Live #136

Inside you is music. Melodies both familiar and brand-new. Your body twitches, stretches, contracts and expands in constant interpretation. The notes tumble out of you. Every sentence is a song, every movement is a dance. When you finally accept your role of composer and choreographer you go from being an exploited natural resource to being a prodigy. You are an unconscious genius, swirling inside with notions, inventions and stirring symphonies. Harness these random rhythms and share your vision. Be Mozart, be Picasso, be the unfettered, unafraid artist that we all secretly are. Awaken and arise. And invite us to dance to your tune.

Rikki Beadle-Blair

Reasons to Live #137

Whether you were planned or accidental, you are a unique and thrilling collision of nature's powers. Whether or not you know or knew your mother, she is there in your eyes. Whether you fall or fly, you still have another chance to be her tiptoe, her dance or her stamp on the world. Whether or not she is proud of you, you can be proud of yourself in her name. Whether or not she understands and appreciates you, you can determine to celebrate her and strive to understand and appreciate yourself. Whether you were brought up, dragged up or pushed up, you come from life. And every day can be a tribute to that. Starting with today. Love your mother, love your source. It all flows from there.

Rikki Beadle-Blair

Reasons to Live #138

With each challenge we encounter, we are offered a clear choice. To grow from experience, or to shrink from it. It all comes down to whether we are prepared to acknowledge that choice and what we decide to do with it. Suffering does not come from pain, but our rejection of it. You may feel beaten but you need never be defeated. Next time you feel provoked, insulted, cheated, wounded or disrespected, take an aerial view of your life, look at the big picture and ask yourself, 'Do I want to shrink or do I want to grow?' and make your choice.

Rikki Beadle-Blair

Reasons to Live #139

The landscapes of our lives are populated with inspiration. You needn't even step out of the door to find that artists, entrepreneurs, scientists, historians, reporters and investigator are everywhere. Your life is bursting with brilliant minds and vibrant voices. Your day is crammed with muses and bright ideas. Don't resist the creative call, pick up your pen, your sketchpad, your computer, your instrument and bear witness, pay tribute to your deep powers of insight or the surface beauty that surrounds you. Initiate debate, instigate justice, insist on change. Strum out your demands, spray-paint your rebellious spirit across the canvas of your day. Sing your personal contribution to the L word. Remind the rest of us that you here. Tell us what you know and what you want to know. Share what you see and show the world the seer you are and the visionary that we all can be.

Rikki Beadle-Blair

Reasons to Live #140

Love is always available. Not the movie kind, not the dream kind. The real kind. The kind of love that builds up and does not break down. The kind of love strong enough to offer without expectation and receive without complication. The kind of love confident enough to be affectionate without hesitation, to accept refusal without feeling rejection - to love anyway and move forward. Not in hope but in the insistence of embracing life. Love that refuses to go to war. Love that celebrates the independence of others. Love that appreciates that connection does not require us to look, think, or desire the same. Love that learns. Love that teaches. Love that embraces. Love that liberates. Love with roots. Love that grows. A solid love that can stretch and bend. Love that always has enough to share. Love that replenishes itself and never runs dry, because it flows from the earth and everything around. A love that springs from you. You are the source of all the love in your world. You are the spring. Let yourself flow, and love will grow all around you.

Rikki Beadle-Blair

Reasons to Live #141

Every crime that you witness offers a chance for insight. Every pain you experience offers an opening for empathy. Each mistake you encounter offers opportunity for understanding. The deeper the bruising the deeper the healing. Everything in your life is here to make you stronger, wiser, kinder, more patient, more dynamic, more alive. You are constructed from experience – use it to build something beautiful and brave.

Rikki Beadle-Blair

Reasons to Live #142

You are young. Whatever the numbers, if you are here, you are not there yet. If you are conscious, you are still a child of life. Still reaching, still stumbling, still exploring, still discovering. It's never too late to learn something new. It's never too late to learn from your mistakes. Never too early to offer peace. You are never too old to salvage friendships, never too twisted to open your arms to love. However long you've been wandering you are never too lost to get back on course, never too far gone to find your way home, never too depleted to be creative, never too broken to mend. Be a little less afraid, less rigid, less vague. Be as young as you are, and only as old as you need to be. The journey still lies before you and you are only at the beginning.

Rikki Beadle-Blair

Reasons to Live #143

You are beautiful. Not just for someone your age, not just for someone your size or shape - just beautiful. Not only spiritually - physically. Beauty is not in the eye of the beholder, it's right there in your face, in your body, your step, your style, in your reach. Stop searching in the mirror for what others have. Look at what you have. You are filled to the brim and coated head-to-toe with heartbreaking miraculous beauty. Beauty is not restricted to what's contemporary or classical, it's not dictated by what's popular. Beauty is not owned by magazines and million dollar ad campaigns, beauty is yours and, by its very nature, entirely free. Beauty is not a fashion, it's not a trick of the light or Photoshop. You can make yourself prettier, you can make yourself fitter and that's wonderful. But it doesn't change the fact that you are already beautiful right now, unadorned, exactly as you are – and when you build on that foundation of truth, there is no height you cannot attain, no heavenly body you cannot reach. Share your beauty generously, wilfully, shamelessly, with everyone lucky enough to come into contact with you. Reclaim your reflection, and let the world see your beautiful face.

Rikki Beadle-Blair

Reasons to Live #144

The world is waiting. For you, with all your genius, your radiance, your lightness and your weight. For you, with all your wisdom and naiveté, your clumsiness and grace. You with all your lumps and bumps and scars, secret screw-ups and complex history. You with all your laziness and craziness, your clichés, your innovations, your oops, your wow, your hair, skin, muscle, sinew, bones, flesh and fat. All of you, every cubic inch of you, every thought and theory in you, every blink, every bruise, every twitch, every sniff, every laugh, every sigh, every sob, every yell, every breath. Give all of yourself, invest yourself, interest yourself, interrogate yourself, confess yourself, release yourself. Offer yourself to life without reservation. Generously, healthily, affectionately. Fall into the arms of life. Explore the world, pay tribute. And let the world explore your heart and mind and find itself there. The world is waiting - arms open - ready for you. So what are you gonna do?

Rikki Beadle-Blair

Reasons to Live 145

Let the past be the past. Abandon the search for the mythical beast of 'closure' and start concentrating on openings. Instead of struggling to heal history, why not channel resources into making today as healthy as it can possibly be? If the road has been rocky, why go over it again? Don't get stuck waiting for apologies and explanations you don't need. Don't look behind you to find the way forward. Step ahead into the light. You can't change what's done but you can transform what is. This moment is yours to mould.

Rikki Beadle-Blair

Reasons to Live #146

Those who really love you will speak the truth with gentle clarity. Those who love you will listen and try to hear you. They will not make you weak by spoiling you, they will not presume to try and strengthen you through aggression. They will defend you from your self-destruction but ultimately respect your right to make your own choices. They will be there in all seasons and all weathers, to encourage your ambitions, and refuse to indulge your weak excuses. They will not hurt you, lie to you or restrain you from life. They will love you. They will respect you. But only as much as you love and respect yourself. And there is so much to love. So many of nature's miracles reside in you and all of humanity's potential. Be gentle, loving and strong with your gifts. Be thankful for your bounty and make the most of all you are. Be gratitude. Be grace. Be love. Be loving. Be beloved. Be loved.

Rikki Beadle-Blair

Reasons to Live #147

Whatever you think is guiding you - fate or God or random chance - you still need to look after yourself. Whether you believe in magic or muscle or Machiavellian manipulation, it's all for nothing if you're not around to reap the results. You don't have to feel like crap in the morning to have fun; you don't have to feel like crap at all. You don't have to let your teeth rot or your digestion go to hell. You don't need to stress yourself out to feel alive. You can choose kind lovers, gravitate to supportive friends, determine to drink smart and drive sober, eat well, exercise a little and constantly expand your mind. Look after yourself and help your angels.

Rikki Beadle-Blair

Reasons to Live #148

You are the boss. You alone run your awesome empire. No one can make you do anything you truly don't want to. If a gun is to your head and you hand over your shoes, that's self-preservation – that's a choice. It's pointless to disrespect that choice by denying or decrying it. Where you work, and who you work with or for is, in the end, your decision. If you are single, it's because you are choosy, however limited you believe your choices to be. The limits are in you alone. You do not have to wait to be asked. You can instigate. You do not have to live in dark confusion, you can investigate. You do not need to be saved, you can save yourself. Suffering does not have to be the price of survival. You can live every moment at your disposal in compliant or defiant celebration. You do not need to be paralysed, you can make a move. The only move that counts is in your mind. You are never out of options, you can always choose. And you always do. Every day. You choose to pay rent. You choose to share or live alone. You choose to be early, late or on time. To agree or disagree with what you are told, what you read and what you have always believed. Your life is in service of your vision. The result of your resolutions. The response to your level of sacrifice. The solid-state proof of your commitment. This is your kingdom and there can be a revolution at any moment. Any moment you choose.

Rikki Beadle-Blair

Reasons to Live #149

Whatever your natural gifts, no one ever ran a marathon by accident. To run in the finals, to stand on the podium, to take home the gold, you have to perspire, to persist, to push yourself. Birth is all the luck we'll ever need. Once you're grown, the rest is up to you. Find and refine your skills, find your teachers and trainers, find your peers, find your passion and drive. Cosiness is a killer. Give yourself something to get up and get out the house for. There's freedom and joy in the pursuit of purpose. The secret to success is in your sweat.

Rikki Beadle-Blair

Reasons to Live #150

You are an artist. Whether you want to be or not, it comes so naturally to you. You speak and there's the music, you move and there's the dance. It's as natural to you as breathing. Choreographer, composer, journalist, clown, presenter, entertainer, investigator, muse, there's no limit to you. Whether freelance or employee, your true vocation is unavoidable: a lifelong commitment to work-in-progress. You are a creative with breathtaking raw talent, with unlimited capacity to enlighten and entertain; with all that it takes to change the world. Your only real choices are in actively how to run your business. To discover how to harness these passionate primitive gestures and consciously, decisively, make a life.

Rikki Beadle-Blair

Reasons to Live #151

Art is in everything. In every encounter, every experience, every transaction, every discovery, every mundane regular object, action or occurrence, creativity nestles, waiting with monumental patience to rescue you. And once you see the potential for birth in everything, death will not frighten you, criticism will not faze you, age will not concern you, solitude will not isolate you, loss will not diminish you only enrich you. Once you see the potential in everything, including the disintegration of your expectations, the world will not terrorize, only inspire you, and fulfilment will no longer be elusive – it will hold you in both hands like a posy and bloom you into bouquets. You will see roses in your wounds, and the child in the face of the angry aggressors. And you will write love songs to adversaries and restore us all to grace.

Rikki Beadle-Blair

Reasons to Live #152

You don't need to be tough to be strong. If you are loving, gentle, and open enough you can survive almost anything. You don't have to cling to cynicism as a defence: the greatest protection in this world is an open mind and resourceful spirit. It's not necessary to defeat anyone to achieve victory. You don't need to inflict hurt to heal yourself. You are brave enough to be vulnerable and innocent enough to be naked without shame. You are secure enough to risk betrayal, assured in the knowledge that as long are you remain true to yourself you are unassailable.

Rikki Beadle-Blair

Reasons to Live #153

Everything is amazing. Each thing in existence stunningly complex in its composition yet simple in its existence. The way that everything eventually dissolves to contribute to the creation of everything else. That billions of identical molecules gather in such infinite, individual and unrepeatable combinations is a miracle. Nothing is boring, everything is brand-new and brilliant. Everything you see around you is a firework display. And you yourself are as awesome as the Great Barrier Reef, as breathtaking as the Aurora Borealis, you are evidence of the scale of nature's ambition, you are a living, breathing wonder of the world. And you can do amazing things. You are already doing amazing things. Because you are, quite simply, amazing.

Rikki Beadle-Blair

Reasons to Live #154

Your talent is not a secret, don't keep it to yourself for a moment longer. Don't be afraid of your capabilities. Don't be ashamed of your ambition. Don't be shy of who you are. You don't have to shout about it, just put it out there for the world to see and the all hungering beasts and birds will gather at your door. Your beauty is not a secret. Don't keep your treasure locked away – people need your radiance to light up their own troves and remind them of their riches. The law of attraction is not a secret. What you give you get, and when you withhold yourself you cheat yourself along with everyone else. If you want to prosper, then share; if you want to be loved, be lovely. If you want to connect with others, connect with yourself.

Rikki Beadle-Blair

Reason to Live #155

You are not a robot. It's human to be tired, it's okay to be a little emotional, it's acceptable and understandable to admit you need a break. For a muscle to grow, it needs a combination of stress and rest. So give yourself a moment, give yourself space and sustenance. Take time to take stock, to assess progress, review, refuel, regroup or just switch off and have yourself some good old-fashioned fun. Don't forget you're meant to be enjoying life. Do what's needed to pull it together and move on up the mountain. The higher you climb, the better the view. Don't forget to turn and take it in.

Rikki Beadle-Blair

Reasons to Live #156

Whatever happens, whatever twists and turns occur or mistakes we make, fruitless crushes, painful clashes, frustrating knock-backs, blank refusals, confusions, misrepresentations, misunderstandings... the one thing we need never sacrifice is our grace. Full participation in your life will bring you out into variable weather. You will be fired, you will be ignored, you will be insulted, over-looked, undervalued, you will be side-lined, you will be relegated, you will be dumped. And you will be noticed, you will be approached, you will be touched. And through it all, to process failure or survive success, poverty or wealth, all you will need will be the grace you were born with and faith in the grace of others.

Rikki Beadle-Blair

Reasons to Live #157

You don't have to enter into the drama. When emotions run high and reactions run amok, you don't have to respond in kind. Instead of feeding the fire, you can put your ego to one side and simply address the facts: what are the needs, what are the stakes, and how can you get through this and back on track. You don't always have to convince people you're the good guy, you don't always need to prove that you're right. It's not always necessary to try and control what others think, feel or do. You can calmly weigh and address their concerns and your own and then move on. Decide how you want to live your life – in conflict or in resolution. Use your energy for healing not wounding. Don't obsess on defeat. Concern yourself only with forward motion. Move on.

Rikki Beadle-Blair

Reasons to Live #158

You can change your mind. As any athlete knows, it's crucial to train and tune your body, but what gives you the edge is how you think. If you are in a rut, the rut is in your mind. If you are in a trap, that trap is in your thinking. What others think, say or do has almost no power over you. What truly governs your life and maps your course are your value system, your habitual thought patterns, your emotional responses. Put your efforts into retraining your brain and you can transform your body, your relationships, your career, your circumstances, your income and your outcome. Take control of your brain. Decide how you want to live. Then decide how you want to think. Free your thinking and you free everything. Change your mind and you change your life.

Rikki Beadle-Blair

Reasons to Live #159

Disregard others and you disregard experience. Dismiss others and you swindle yourself. Everyone has something to teach you. Everyone is an education. Instead of trying to be better than everyone, look at all the ways in which they're smarter, kinder, more talented than you and let them inspire you to reach their brilliance and beyond. Let them know how great they are. Encourage a world of wonders. No-one living is unable to leave a mark. Each and everyone on this earth is a work of art and a great and influential artist. Not just potentially but actually. Sparks of stunning or subtle brilliance are in every one of us - none are exempt. See the genius in everyone you meet and you will find the genius in you.

Rikki Beadle-Blair

Reasons to Live #160

It's okay to include yourself. It's not arrogant to pay yourself a compliment. It's not madness to appreciate your attractiveness. It's not self-indulgent to give yourself some attention. Every opportunity to look after others is a blessing and should be treasured, but you are in the world too. You are vulnerable too. You need love and support and pampering and a good talking to, just like everyone does. If the lifeboat has a leak it can't save anyone. Find time to rest, to venture, to explore, to recharge, to be loved. You deserve your attention. Put yourself back on your schedule.

Rikki Beadle-Blair

Reasons to Live #161

Sometimes it's good to stray off course. Now and then the wild thing inside you cries out to be released and compassion demands that you let it roam. Every once in a while you have to close your eyes and leap into the thrill of the unknown. Occasionally it's crucial to do something crazy and seize the tail of adventure. Absolute certainty is the death of art. There's no win without risk. Every day is all gambles anyway, why not throw the dice yourself once in a while? Why not stray away from the firelight and dance with the shadows? Why not sail over the horizon in search of new worlds? Why not shuffle the schedule and shock yourself awake? Why not raise your heart-rate? Why not be young? Why not live a little? Why not live a lot?

Rikki Beadle-Blair

Reasons to Live #162

You get going. You get lost. You get nowhere. You keep going. You finally get somewhere - it's not how you imagined it - you keep going. You change direction. Keep going. You stumble into storms, tear yourself on thorns, get swept up in twisters, ambushed by bandits, accosted by beggars - you give what you can spare and keep going. You make mistakes, make amends, make love, make music, make babies, make trouble, make magic, make haste, make judgements, make a spectacle, make an almighty fool of yourself – you keep going. You lose yourself in hell, confuse yourself with fleeting false glimpses of heaven. You keep going. Hit the peak of the mountain and the view is breathtaking. Lightning strikes and everything is illuminated. There's a natural disaster and everything is devastated. The sun breaks through – gone again – but it will return – to set again and rise again and again and again – and so will you. You keep going. Until you've seen all, tasted all, been all that you know you can be at least once. Until you've experienced every kind of ordinary and astounding you were born to be. You get lazy, you get crazy, you get inspired and exhausted, you get battered and bloody. You use up every breath this brave body has to offer until at last it lets you move on – and you keep going. Because life is wonderful and you are full of wonders. Because you must. Keep going.

Rikki Beadle-Blair

Reasons to Live #163

You are the living embodiment of one belief system: your own. A human testament to all you've achieved and everything you've bailed on. You represent your morality, your fears, your scepticism and your faith. You are the sum total of your procrastinations, your excuses, your addictions and your phobias, along with your conviction, your dedication, your imagination, your accumulating wisdom and your willingness to learn and grow. The confidence others have shown or not shown in you is worth nothing compared to your confidence in yourself. That's where the work must be done. That is where your story is decided. This is the fate that you have made, the future you are building. This is what you have dared, this is what you have settled for, this is how far you have drifted, how shrewdly you have sailed. You stand for something. For human possibility - and possibility is built from consistency and commitment. Commit to yourself, stand up for yourself. As no other can.

Rikki Beadle-Blair

Reasons to Live #164

Nothing could be more wonderful than to know whenever you move on from this world, that you lived here with every conscious fibre of you. To be sure that you gave yourself entirely to the things you cared about and lived a life that was fuelled by love. To treasure your failings for what they are - beautiful leaves that fell from you and fertilized the earth you grow from. To be certain that you were never lazy in your passions, never stingy with your affections or blind to fortune. That you did not wait on miracles but instigated them. That you met bitterness with generosity, cynicism with understanding, and faced fear with a boundless sense of fun. To know in your heart that you were a true friend and a sincere lover. To believe that you were kind. To hope that you were helpful. honest and truthful. To feel certain in your soul that you committed to the freedom you were born with and lived a real life. To know that you were real.

Rikki Beadle-Blair

Reasons to Live #165

Sometimes you have to stop thinking and just do. You've read all the writings. You've done the research; studied your subject, learned your craft, trained yourself, honed your brain. Then comes the time to stop worrying and just trust yourself. Stop surviving and start living. Stop planning and be. Stop the mind-chatter and start listening to the pump of your blood and just let yourself be who are you are, where you are, living this life through this breath, then this breath, doing what you love, loving what you do and working with what you have. Life is not an idea. It's an activity. Living is in the doing.

Rikki Beadle-Blair

Reasons to Live #166

Each day is a fresh invitation to everything: a call to live in the world on every available level - the physical and the spiritual, the conceptual and the practical, the emotional and the intellectual, the solid and the shifting. You are as layered as life, as brilliant as Einstein, as empathic as Gandhi, as romantic as Shakespeare, as inventive as Edison, as insightful as Buddha, as creative as creation itself. You are equal to every living organism, entirely as intricate and as thrillingly imperfect, and every single cell in you is crying out to be of service to the universe. Forget about the illusion of your limitations, put aside your timid ideas of what you are allowed to attempt or expected to achieve. You are not just a speck in the grand scheme of things – you are the grand scheme of things. You are a genius, you are a prophet, you are a ground-breaking step in evolution. You are living breathing potential, and you were born to change the world. You are significant. And you are here. Be entirely here; entirely awake, entirely present, entirely involved, entirely alive. Be yourself unlimited and give your unlimited self to life.

Rikki Beadle-Blair

Reasons to Live #167

No one compares with you, because you are incomparable. No one can compete with you - you are in a league of your own. Don't waste a second wishing for any part of anyone else. If you want something, work for it. If you can't change yourself, make peace with yourself and truly make advances. Get on with the thrilling mission of being the most fulfilled version of you. You have no flaws, just evidence of your humanity. You have no competitors or opponents, just mirrors and muses. Let them go to war alone without you and do battle with themselves. Leave them to their struggle as you embark on your own powerful, crusade of purpose and love.

Rikki Beadle-Blair

Reasons to Live #168

Who would you be if you decided to let nothing stop you? What would be achieved if you got out of your own way? What would happen if you mined your capacity for discipline and redefined your sense of fun? What if you rested well, drank wisely, ate powerfully, got up early and got things done? What if you refused to waste another second on feeling sorry for yourself? If you took every ounce of energy spent on resentment and poured it into movement? What if you abandoned anger, frustration, disappointment and fear to focus on freedom? What if you found a way to love everyone and everything and made appreciation your mission? What if you decided that your talent was not a secret. How would it be if everyone - especially you - knew that, whatever comes your way, you will use it as rocket fuel? What if people looked at you and all they could see was light? What if success was your brand? Who knows what you could do? You do.

Rikki Beadle-Blair

Reasons to Live #169

Fulfilment is not just for other people, it's for everyone. Stop calling out for happiness to be delivered and make your own. It's healthier and safer and more satisfying when you know what's gone into what you're getting. Stop looking enviously at what's on other people's plates and start savouring what's on yours. Your family, your peers, career or love-life cannot make you happy - only your appreciation of them can. Nothing is more uplifting than the realisation that happiness is in your own hands. Nothing is more energizing than taking ownership of your circumstances. Nothing is more delicious than the decision to take full control.

Rikki Beadle-Blair

Reasons to Live #170

It's amazing how often we already know the answers to our trickiest questions. We can be brilliant at slyly distracting ourselves from our own dilemmas through daily displays of knowledge and dispensing of wisdoms, freely giving out the advice we so badly need to take ourselves. Sometimes happiness is just a simple case of practising what we preach and learning what we teach. Progress begins with having both humility and the confidence to admit that you already hold all the solutions but are lacking application. The breakthrough comes when you realise that you are special but not original – that you are your own angel and your own devil; that your problems are universal and that you can stand in judgement over no other; that you are human; that your saviour is staring you in the face every morning in the mirror. Life changes require thought changes. Seeing the light takes insight. Satisfaction comes from taking action. Wisdom is knowing when it's time to take your own advice.

Rikki Beadle-Blair

Reasons to Live #171

It's so simple. You can resolve to stop throwing your power at opposing forces and start saving your precious energy for love. Doing the work you love, investing in a home you love, eating the food you love rather than the food that's easy to find and swallow.... and loving - really loving - the people you love. Commitment to love can be scary – it may require change. But there is nothing to fear. Love is not painful, love is not selfish, love is not draining, love is not drama, love is not lazy, love is not habit. Love can be demanding, but always gives as much as it gets. Love is simple when you let it be. Love is truthful, love is gentle, love is kind. Love is worth it. You know love when you let yourself see it. All you have to do is open your eyes. Focus on love, and when you find it share your love with the world. Let it be easy. Let it be simple. Let it be all about love.

Rikki Beadle-Blair

Reasons to Live #172

When something looks like a problem, turn it round and find the lesson. What is this situation really for? To teach you? To humble you? To strengthen you? Is this circumstance an invitation to rest and recover or rise up in revolution? Every event in life, however gleaming or grim comes with an offer. And the offer is love. Love is not for the faint-hearted. It takes courage and vision. If you can find the way to see what's on offer and respond with grace and strength and truth, you find the way to success in its purest form. And a life of love.

Reasons to Live #173

This is the most important day of your life. Because, right now, it's all you have. Whether it offers earthquakes or traumas - physical or emotional - or the exact same unbroken daily routine; whether you seize it or cradle it, accept it or reject it, follow the familiar furrow or turn your plough around; whether you decide it's time to make changes, big or small, or to accept and embrace your life exactly as it is - this day - your day - belongs to you and you alone. And what you do with it defines you.

Rikki Beadle-Blair

Reasons to Live #174

Only you can worry you. Only you can frighten you. Only you can hurt you. Only you can break your heart. Only you can distract you. Only you can delay you, only you can defeat you. Only you can make you feel awkward. Only you can make you feel strange. The same you that can make you feel strong. The same you that can make you feel young. The one and only one who can take you forward, the same you that can make the most of everything you have and all that you are. Everyone else is an excuse. You are the only reason. Give yourself the gift of yourself and the world is yours.

Rikki Beadle-Blair

Reasons to Live #175

There are no problems, only puzzles. And one of the greatest is how to achieve balance: How to stretch ourselves without hurting ourselves. How to respect ourselves without judging others. How to find confidence without arrogance and tap into our determination without becoming a tyrant. How to improve ourselves without falling into self-hatred. It can done. We can eat healthy and still find flavour, we can take ourselves seriously and still have fun. We can be powerful and humble, loving and firm, honest and tactful, sensitive and resilient. It's a beautiful balancing act: learning how to work and rest, think and feel, conform and rebel, demand and respect, give and take. We can be a little of everything and entirely individual. The key to the solution is to love the puzzle. The answer to life is, as ever, to decline invitations to conflict, and love and respect everything - including our obstacles and including ourselves.

Rikki Beadle-Blair

Reasons to Live #176

If your freedom depends on anyone else's permission you will keep yourself incarcerated. If your wealth is contingent on what the world can spare then you will find yourself a beggar. If your beauty craves acceptance then it will never fully bloom. If you seek validation in external appreciation, then you will never know romance. If you subscribe to the myth of luck, you will never find your fortune. Take full possession of yourself and trust yourself to live an independent life and you will find true connection to everything and everyone, regardless of what they say or do. Speak to the world in your own voice and the answer will come calling out of everything and everyone - 'this is true love - this is real life - truly lived.'

Rikki Beadle-Blair

Reasons to Live #177

Best times come when you don't know what on earth to do next. That's when the call for resourcefulness, resilience and persistence is the loudest. Those magic times when you're forced out of cosy complacency into the hot sun or the driving rain to take your place in the world as a pioneer; to revisit your original passion and update it to tackle the requirements of current circumstances; when it's time to dig deep and come up with a fresh approach that pays deeper respect to your soul's intention; when it's time to stop sleepwalking and get real. So, when the money runs out, the phone doesn't ring, the house burns down or your desire is unrequited - say thank you for the freedom and answer the call to get creative.

Rikki Beadle-Blair

Reasons to Live #178

With so much always on offer boredom is constantly revealed to be a choice. Disappointment is a word for our unwillingness to engage with the beauty of the present moment and its endless possibilities. Failure takes strenuous commitment to doing nothing. Success simply requires you to appreciate things as they are. With every step you arrive somewhere. With every day you are born a little more.

Rikki Beadle-Blair

Reasons to Live #179

You will not find your strength in conformity. You will not build a fulfilling future from an imitation of someone else's life. You will not find safety in numbers, only obscurity. Confusion comes rushing in when you hide who you are in the vain hope of gaining acceptance. Power lies in trusting your own singular combination of qualities. Freedom comes from commitment to your individual vision for your life. Independence is not loneliness. You will only find your true connection to everything when you feel secure enough to be authentic. It's not necessary to fool anyone, you don't have to hide, you don't need to lie. Liberty comes from letting go of fear of yourself. Peace comes from honouring your essence. Happiness come self-acceptance. Progress begins with truth.

Rikki Beadle-Blair

Reasons to Live #180

In the end, it's all about what you make happen. There will be twists and turns, wild weather and unpredicted storms, but complete surprises are relatively rare. You can decide to be the next surprise in your story. You can be the next twist in your tale. If you don't like things as they are - in your world, in your life, in your mind - you can choose do something about it. You can make a noise. You can make a stand. You can make a difference. Your choices are what got you here, your choices are what keep you here, your choices will take you wherever you go next. Life is tough sometimes. But so are you. That's why you're still around. Inaction is an active decision and it defines your life. You can't control others, but you can control yourself and your own startlingly-complex, stunningly simple beautiful little part of the universe. You are at your own mercy and you can rescue yourself any moment you choose.

Rikki Beadle-Blair

Reasons to Live #181

We are all slaves to our addictions. When you are hooked you will steal, you will sell yourself, you will stop at nothing to feed your habit. Once you replace coffee, cigarettes or compulsive random sex with creativity, contribution and human connection, there is almost nothing you can conceive that you can't achieve. The trick is to discover what really gives you the healthiest happiest high and then give yourself over to that. Addictions are not accidental - you have to pick up the pipe or the pint in the first place. You can select a constructive addiction. You can commit to what works for you. You can give your life to yourself.

Rikki Beadle-Blair

Reasons to Live #182

If you wait for permission to begin your adventure, you'll spend your whole life waiting. Permission is no-one else's to give, stop saddling others with false burdens. You don't need permission to be an artist, you don't need permission to become a scholar, adventurer or entrepreneur. It's a contradiction to apply for authorization to try something radical. It's ludicrous to hope for permission to be a revolutionary. Don't use those you care for as excuses. If no-one is wounded, then no-one's a problem. Consult with those who you care for, but don't pretend the conclusions you live by are anyone's but your own. Make your own blend of traditional and liberal, give yourself permission to read and write what you want, wear what you want, say what you want, work how you want or want what you want. Encourage yourself to venture out into the world, allow yourself to discover your spiritual home. Be as black, brown, yellow or white as feels authentic, as male or female as you fancy, as specific or ambiguous as you feel. Choose your personal mix-tape of stereotypes and quirks, your own individual taste in music, movies, crushes and passions. You can't get a valid permit to be yourself from anyone except you. And you can grant it to yourself whenever you're ready.

Rikki Beadle-Blair

Reasons to Live 183

The last thing you need to be is perfect. Literally. If you achieve perfection, you might as well die, because it's over. Having something to strive for gives you something to do. You are a builder, you are a gardener, you are a chef - and you are the tower, the flowerbed, the banquet. You are your life's work, learning and relearning, rethinking, reconsidering. You are learning so much - and most of it's about yourself. Be thankful that you don't know it all yet and relish excavating your hidden wonders. Enjoy your quirky face and your moments of awkwardness along with your wild rash rushes of brazenness, your lightning strikes of inspiration and random brilliant insights. Carve your own cleft in the rock of the world and don't be too shy when others come to visit. Be proud of your oddness, be patient with your frailties, strive for understanding of your inconsistencies - they bear witness to your complex history and they are waiting to be integrated and mated to give birth to your unique character. You don't need to look like anyone else to be beautiful. You don't need to think like anyone else to be brilliant. And you don't have to be perfect to be worthwhile. Just here. And you've achieved that already.

Rikki Beadle-Blair

Reasons to Live 184

Perfectionism is procrastination: "If chapter one is not perfect, how could I write a whole book?" "If my body is not perfect, why would I have a healthy love-life?" "If others are not behaving perfectly in return, what's the point in me making an effort?" "If this moment is not exactly as I envisaged it, how can I enjoy it?" "If the weather is not perfect, why should I leave the house?" There are two perfections available: the fact and the myth. The perfection in your mind is a fiction constructed from your heavily-edited projected view of the world. In reality absolutely everything is a perfect outcome of contributing factors with an infinite and spectacular potential for expansion. Pursuit of improvement is powerful. Pining for perfection is paralyzing. Growth, learning, stumbling, searching, stretching, discovering, being wounded and healed are all glorious adventures in this eternally expanding and evolving universe. And it's all available to you whenever you're ready to admit that you're tough enough to risk a little vulnerability. Why settle for mere perfection, when you deserve something better?

Rikki Beadle-Blair

Reasons to Live #185

You don't need to numb yourself to every possibility of pain. You don't always need be comfortable. You are not required to get off your face to find your smile. You don't have to retreat to alternative states to get fresh perspectives. You don't need to blur yourself to avoid the world. You can survive moments of awkwardness, you can enjoy not having all the answers. You don't need to appear seamless and invulnerable to have strength or significance in the world. Every toddler knows there's no shame in falling when learning how to get around. When you over-protect yourself, you cheat yourself. When you hide yourself, you lose yourself. You don't have to barricade the world out, you don't have to live under a bell-jar. You can be peaceful and cope with conflict, you can be sober and face the truth, you can speak your mind and change your mind as you learn and turn and grow. You can be clear-headed and clear-sighted enough to embrace critiques that help and discard opinions that harm. You can get high on clarity and you can handle reality. You can survive the world as it is and exactly as you are. Because you are strong. And you do belong.

Rikki Beadle-Blair

Reasons to Live #186

You don't have to mess around a moment longer. If you want a great role you can write one. If you want to be fitter you can find a trainer. If you want to raise your game you can find the right team. You can define your own family. You can say I love you without fear or expectation or shame. You can refuse to perpetuate disrespectful alliances. You can refuse to be bitter. You can refuse to sulk. You can let go of frustration and confusion and channel that energy into brainstorming and action. You can stop wondering why people don't do what they say and do it yourself. You can say thank you for every little thing that comes your way. You can understand that, no matter who calls themselves your boss, you ultimately run your own business. You can learn new skills. You can capitalize on your knowledge. You can be your own Santa Claus and write a letter to yourself. You can be your own guardian angel and keep yourself safe. You can be your own saint and make your own miracles. You can hit the wall and you can recover. You can move on. You can defy detractors. You can confound critics. You can survive yourself. You can find the confidence it takes to tame your ego. You can realise that tomorrow is already here and ride into the sunset with yourself. You can fall back in love with today.

Rikki Beadle-Blair

Reasons to Live #187

What you say has impact. What you do is defining. What you feel is real. But at the root of all of this is what and how you think. If you have to work on one thing in order to change everything, work on your mind. Once you change the way you think, the way you experience the world will transform beyond all expectation, and so will the way world responds to you. It's not easy – thought-patterns are sensitive, skittish creatures of habit, and harnessing them takes vision, clarity and persistent love - but your thoughts are also secret superheroes, and when you are ready to call on them they will swoop in and save you. If you can train your brain to see the truth and the potential in everything inside and surrounding you, then there is almost nothing worth doing that you can't do. The mind is mightier than any living circumstance. And so are you.

Rikki Beadle-Blair

Reasons to Live #188

If you have a vision some will call you crazy. If you refuse to be reined in, people will call you wild. It's themselves they fear: the judgement they feel whenever you refuse to justify their choices. Follow your passions and some will say you're selfish. If you show your love and appreciation, others will call you false. If you hold nothing back you'll be labelled self-indulgent. If you commit to love, they'll call you deluded. Generosity will be met with suspicion, innocence with cynicism, both ambition and humility with envy and scorn. Many will criticize - they'll whisper and shake their heads and laugh. They'll tell you the proper way to do things they themselves have never done. But none of them are you. This is your vision, your passion, your story, and when you reach the end no-one will thank you for living your life their way. There is a world within you, with oceans to dive into and jungles to explore. If you die climbing your mountain, it won't be fear that took your life. If you dare to live in the fullness of your truest, most creative self, nothing will take your life. Such a life can never be taken. Only envied or shared. Or lived.

Rikki Beadle-Blair

Reasons to Live #189

You wake up every morning extravagantly ambitious for the day. You're going to be athletic, cook imaginatively, eat healthily, at the same time as reading a whole book while writing a short story, a poem, a song and a blog. You're going to manage your money better, rearrange the house, sort out that cupboard, pay attention to your skin, lose 2 pounds, answer every email, give your neglected loved ones all the attention they need without looking at your watch, commit 3 random acts of kindness, be great at business, sort out your love-life and dress like a dream. So then when you realise within the hour that you are not going to manage to tick every item on your list, how do you stop yourself from crashing down in flames of failure and self-contempt? Do what you can - as wholeheartedly as you can, as simply, honestly and realistically as you can. One thing at a time with all your focus, fire and sense of fun. Then on to the next thing and go to bed excited by tomorrow and all the things you've still got to do. Decide that whatever happens, tomorrow is going to be a great day. Just like today. Because whether you notice or not, it is.

Rikki Beadle-Blair

Reasons to Live #190

Integrity is all. No matter what values those around you express, follow or demonstrate, regardless of what pressure is brought to bear, if you can be faithful to your truest self, you will rarely go astray. You will know what jobs to take, you will know what rules to break, you will know what art or love to make. You will not always get the quick fix, you will not be guaranteed the shiny medal, the windfall or applause, but you will never lose sight of the true prize - your realest self. With integrity as your guiding star you will know which paths to walk, what to eat, what to study, which parties to join, which invitations to accept or refuse. Ego will no longer be your dictator feeding you false propaganda, and retaliation and revenge will reveal themselves to be the empty victories and devastating defeats they really are. The truth will not create panic, and you will rarely feel the need to lie to survive. Shame will become a stranger, and the gnawing confusions and distractions of self-hatred and dissatisfaction will finally be calmed. With integrity as your compass you will find your vocation, you will find peace, passion and your deepest connection. With integrity, you will find true love - for you will be true love yourself.

Rikki Beadle-Blair

Reasons to Live #191

Your relationship with yourself, like every other, has to be worked on to flourish. You have to take the time to get to know yourself. Know when to approach yourself with respect and sensitivity and when to beat yourself over the head with a club and seize control. It's vital to realize when it's time to make changes. It's crucial to make the effort to keep things fresh. Romance yourself, take yourself out for special meals and treats, spot yourself across a crowded room and smile at yourself. Compliment yourself and complement yourself. Complete yourself. Spend time listening to your dreams and encourage yourself to make them become realities. Never lie to yourself, don't cheat on yourself, call yourself on your bullshit. Laugh at yourself, but never put yourself down - in public or private. Support yourself. Push yourself. Challenge yourself. Make yourself feel appreciated. It's no one else's duty to value you - that's all extra. Your sense of worth starts entirely with you. You are one of the great loves of your life and this is your love story.

Rikki Beadle-Blair

Reasons to Live #192

Blame is a brutal prison. Blame is the cruellest slave-master. When we blame others, we condemn ourselves. When you decide that someone else is accountable for your suffering, you place them in charge of your happiness and yourself at their disposal. You do not need to be rescued, you do not need to be set free. No one can be saved, only assisted. You don't have to be ruled by your emotions, you do not have to be over-whelmed by your moods. If you can't help how you feel, then no one else can. But the truth is, you can help how you feel. You can refuse to wallow in self-pity. You can be bold enough to stop depending on others to make you feel fortunate and can get on with wallowing in this great big amazing day with its countless infinite options of things to say, think, feel, explore, create. You can dare to embrace each fresh opportunity to take control of your responses. You can fling open the cage door and once again feel the wind in your fur and feathers as you rediscover the wild in you and the child in you. When you let your spirit lead the way you can go anywhere. Anywhere you choose. Because you are in charge. And you hold the keys.

Rikki Beadle-Blair

Reason to Live #193

We know our lives by the company we keep. We know others when we meet their friends. Who are you spending your time with? Creatives or couch surfers? Users or contributors? Whiners or activists? The kind or the cruel? The spiritual or the spiteful? If like attracts like, then what are you like? Old friends should keep you grounded but not hold you back. New friends should inspire, not corrupt you. True friends should focus and not distract you; should encourage you to work and help you to relax. Should know when to laugh at you and when to take you seriously. True friends will be there in a flash when needed, regardless of petty disputes. True friends will tell you what you need to hear, regardless of whether you want to hear it. They will come in and out of orbit like stars and seasons, but they will always be there. Invest in them wholeheartedly and you will never be hungry, poor or alone. Know your friends and you will know yourself.

Rikki Beadle-Blair

Reasons to Live #194

It's always a great day to try something new. Why stay curled up tight in a self-made womb when you can unfurl, open, stretch, and enter the world's embrace? Read something challenging, wear new colours, cuts and cloths, savour new flavours, investigate unexplored genres, experience fresh perspectives, consider challenging points of view. Open your mind and take another look at things you've dismissed. Empathy is an adventure. Understanding is a superpower. An open mind offers the earthbound the yearned-for gift of flight. It's true that nothing expands the mind like travel - are there streets in your neighbourhood you've never walked down? Local adventures you've never considered? Your mind hides untouched pockets aching for a hand. Reach in, reach out. Uncharted continents await your footfall, neglected mountains are calling for your climb. Explore, expand, discover new worlds. Every shadow holds an invitation to the light.

Rikki Beadle-Blair

Reasons to Live #195

Today, like every other, brings the opportunity to live in defiance of limitations. Any time the spirit moves you, you can resolve to be the impossible made possible and empower others to push the boundaries of our humanity. You arrived here against all odds, the sterling achievement of one indefatigable sperm that did what the millions could not. You are living proof of everyday miracles. If you are still breathing then you are still young and life is still before you. Stop wondering what if. Get out there and find fellow trail-blazers to help locate and conquer new creative continents, inspire the hesitant to exceed expectations and redefine our collective capabilities. Cross the tundra, climb the unclimbed, map the unexplored. Do whatever brand-new thing it is that you have yearned to do, be the brand-new thing you were born to be. Dare to be original. Decide to be entirely you. Anything less is cheating the world. Anything less is a tragedy.

Rikki Beadle-Blair

Reasons to Live #196

Success comes not to the most talented, but to those who make the most of the talents they have. True success is defined by happiness and we are at our most happy when doing what we love. Don't let a day go by without following your passion in some way. Don't go to bed without creating something, however small. Make the most of what you have, make the most of what you know, make the most of who you are. Make art, make music, make love, make waves, make a life. Make something happen and don't be shy about it. Share your love with the world, promote your passions. Enjoy your talents fearlessly, persistently and generously and you cannot fail.

Rikki Beadle-Blair

Reasons to Live #197

Passion doesn't wait for permission. While in prison, Jean Genet wrote his first novel on a roll of toilet paper. When the guards tore it to pieces, he got more toilet paper and wrote it again. Achievement does not spring from convenience. When Beethoven went deaf he bit the piano to feel its vibrations through his teeth and wrote his greatest symphony. Art doesn't wait for approval. If you can't find a theatre, build your own stage. If you don't get a gallery, hang your art on trees. Make movies on your smart-phone, project them onto the side of your house. Slap out rhythms on your thighs, stand on street corners and sing. That's what the greats did. They did it anyway. Creativity comes from perspiration not privilege. Genius is a form of madness. Every great work of art is a symptom of autism. Be a little insane. Recklessly express your obsessions. Bare your soul. Risk everything. Fear nothing. Sacrifice luxury. As long as you feed your babies, then nothing else matters. Forget making your parents happy. Forget looking cool to the kids from school. If you fill your life with excuses, you will have an excuse for a life. Art is not an excuse. Art is a reason. Make art anyway. Make art today.

Rikki Beadle-Blair

Reasons to Live #198

Decide to be happy. You don't have to be angry to achieve. You don't need rage to run. You can enjoy every trial. You can acknowledge every tribulation as testament to the fact that you are alive and here in the world. You don't always need to be comfortable. You don't always need to be laughing and carefree. A little pressure is part of the fun and pain can be a treasured teacher. It's hard to see joy in the suffering of others but it is possible to find fulfilment in your ability to be a contributor to their healing. This is not about complacency, this is not about numbing yourself. Your smile is a weapon. It can destroy enemies in a flash and bring you enough energy to change your world. Where there is darkness you can be light. Joy is nuclear. It can rearrange atoms. Nothing is more powerful than a truly positive soul. Nothing is more empowering than the decision to be truly happy. No-one is more unstoppable than those who embrace being truly alive.

Rikki Beadle-Blair

Reasons to Live #199

Beyond every material loss is the possibility of gain. The shedding of possessions is an open invitation to liberation. Just as the end of innocence brings the wealth of experience, and the fading of youth reveals the triumph of survival, peace lies not in the burden of accumulation but in the flexibility and lightness of simplicity. You can relish every moment of living in a world full of miraculous objects, but be aware that you are equal to absolutely everything in existence, owner of no-one, owned by nothing. It's when we can stand naked and empty-handed and still feel our wealth that our lives are richest. It's when we relinquish our fearful attachments that we gain full possession of ourselves.

Rikki Beadle-Blair

Reasons to Live #200

Grace takes strength. To be patient in the face of those who absentmindedly forget their manners takes spiritual muscle. To keep sight of your integrity when those around you abandon their principles requires confidence, clarity and a solid sense of self. To remain steadfastly tender when others panic and attack demands a spirit of understanding, empathy and a profound capacity for love. Like swimming, love takes practice, but once remembered it's the most natural thing in the world. When things fall apart, when the world around you becomes unsure, choose grace. Yes, it takes strength, but you are strong enough.

Rikki Beadle-Blair

Reasons to Live #201

Just as life teaches us repeatedly that the more we learn the less we know, experience offers the delicious revelation that the older we get the younger we become. As life becomes more and more precious when there's less of it to waste; as the value of existence reveals itself and the urgency of our passions make themselves felt; we find ourselves increasingly dwarfed by our own childlike wonder at the world and the stunning variety of everything in it. Let's allow ourselves to be assailed by the individual complexity and universal simplicity of the human heart, and our constant unfolding realisation that we are always at the beginning of our story, still struggling through the birth canal, just getting started, never completed, never grown-up, thrillingly unfulfilled. This is the great unfolding romance: the infant infatuated with living, the radiant baby continually crawling towards the light, the child in you in love with life. Live in tribute to that baby and you will never grow weary. Honour your child and you will never grow old.

Rikki Beadle-Blair

Reasons to Live #202

Be the source of light and the way forward will be illuminated. Be the source of strength and lions will run with you. Be the source of courage and you will be beloved of the brave. Be the source of integrity and you will attract truth. Be the source of understanding and you will initiate epic and intimate communication. Be the source of grace and you will promote peace. Be the source of love and you will see beauty in surprising shadows. Be the source of inspiration and you will be rewarded with that magic that flows from everyone. Embody your desire and you will shift from beggar to benefactor. Stand for hope and you will draw the hopeful to you. Be the things you are looking for in the world and the world will find you.

Rikki Beadle-Blair

Reasons to Live #203

One of the greatest challenges is in meeting our own standards. The hopes and demands we place on others are so often the demands we need to place on ourselves. Can we be as honest, sensitive, understanding, accommodating, diligent, patient, principled and consistent as we would have liked our parents to have been? Can we eat as intelligently, entertain ourselves as responsibly, be as disciplined and free as we hope our children will become? Can we be as smart, sexy, strong and sensitive, supportive and stimulating as our dream partner? Could we love as freely? Be as much fun to be around? Can we be all the things we deserve? Only one soul can answer this. Only one soul can be expected to care enough to try. Be the source of all you want from this world. Become the provider to others of all that you desire. It's always thrilling to have something to strive for. Stop wishing for a better life and start working for it.

Rikki Beadle-Blair

Reasons to Live #204

You are your life. Nothing is more glorious, more thrilling or more freeing than the decision to take utmost and ultimate responsibility for your every action. Nothing is more time-saving, nothing is more life-saving. When you realise that the world is responding to you and become alert to the messages you are sending, you become ready to take control of transforming your relationship with everyone and everything. When you start looking at and listening to both yourself and others with honesty and compassion and genuine interest, you are ready to have real conversations and fruitful exchanges. When you start paying attention, you begin to awaken to possibility. You are ready to create opportunity – to become opportunity – you are ready to be fully alive. And when you are prepared to commit to being increasingly alive, you can begin to live a full life. A life filled with purpose, a life crammed with revelations, a life brimming with a delicious balance of excitement and calm. A life blessed with challenge. A life gifted with learning. A life exploding with magic. A life of alchemy.

Rikki Beadle-Blair